D0052625

BREAKFAST IN·BED

BREAKFAST IN·BED

THE BEST B&B RECIPES FROM NORTHERN CALIFORNIA TO BRITISH COLUMBIA

Carol Frieberg

SASQUATCH BOOKS
Seattle, Washington

Library of Congress Cataloging-in-Publication Data
Breakfast in bed: the best B&B recipes from northern California to British Columbia / edited by Carol Frieberg.
p. cm.
Includes index.
ISBN 0-912365-30-7 : $14.95
1. Breakfast I. Frieberg, Carol, 1959–
TX733.B65 1990 90-40431
641.5'2—dc20 CIP

Front cover photo by Mark Burnside
Food styling by Joan Wickham
Interior illustrations by Jonathan Combs
Designed by Kris Morgan with Jane Jeszeck
Typeset by Scribe Typography

Published by Sasquatch Books
1931 Second Avenue
Seattle, WA 98101

This book is dedicated to all
the special people in my life, each
of whom has added an important
ingredient to this end product—
a labor of love.

TABLE OF CONTENTS

SCONES AND MUFFINS

COFFEE CAKES AND COBBLERS

HOUSE SPECIALTIES

EGG ENTRÉES

CASSEROLES, QUICHES, AND FRITTATAS

FRENCH TOAST, PANCAKES, AND WAFFLES

FRUITS, SAUCES, AND SMOOTHIES

BREADS

INTRODUCTION

Breakfast is a meal with many moods. For some, breakfast means comfort—a hot bowl of oatmeal, a thick slice of cinnamon toast, homemade pancakes—evoking feelings of being warm and cared for. Others enjoy breakfast as a social occasion—a traditional Sunday brunch or an early-morning rendezvous. For the more impulsive, breakfast can be fun and festive—a giant cinnamon roll shared with a friend, breakfast in bed with the Sunday paper, or an exotic meal prepared on the spur of the moment. Still others see breakfast as a quiet time, an opportunity to relax and reflect on the day ahead.

At bed-and-breakfast inns, breakfast takes on a whole new dimension. It's an event full of anticipation, a memory in the making to be savored and remembered.

Just what makes breakfast at a bed and breakfast so special? Perhaps it is simply the love and care with which the food is prepared and served. The breakfasts in your home can be special occasions as well. The meal itself does not have to be elaborate. It simply needs to be presented with flair, flavor, and finesse. A banana is pretty uneventful until it is sliced into a crystal bowl and topped with fresh whipped cream and chopped walnuts. A breakfast of juice, cereal, and coffee appears rather ordinary until it is served in bed with a love note tucked inside the napkin!

The bed-and-breakfast recipes in this book are not difficult to prepare. Many can be made ahead of time, and several can be prepared and frozen for future use. The dishes were chosen for their "creative simplicity," proving that you don't have to be a gourmet cook to serve a gourmet breakfast.

The recipes presented here emphasize fresh, healthy ingredients. Many can be modified to accommodate a low-cholesterol, low-fat diet. They also make use of the bountiful foods native to the Pacific Northwest: berries, fresh seafood, nuts, garden herbs, and grains. All reflect a commitment to excellence by cooks who use the highest-quality ingredients to produce the finest cuisine.

Go ahead and indulge yourself—make each morning count. Experiment, have fun, and remember always to cook with love.

— *Carol Frieberg*

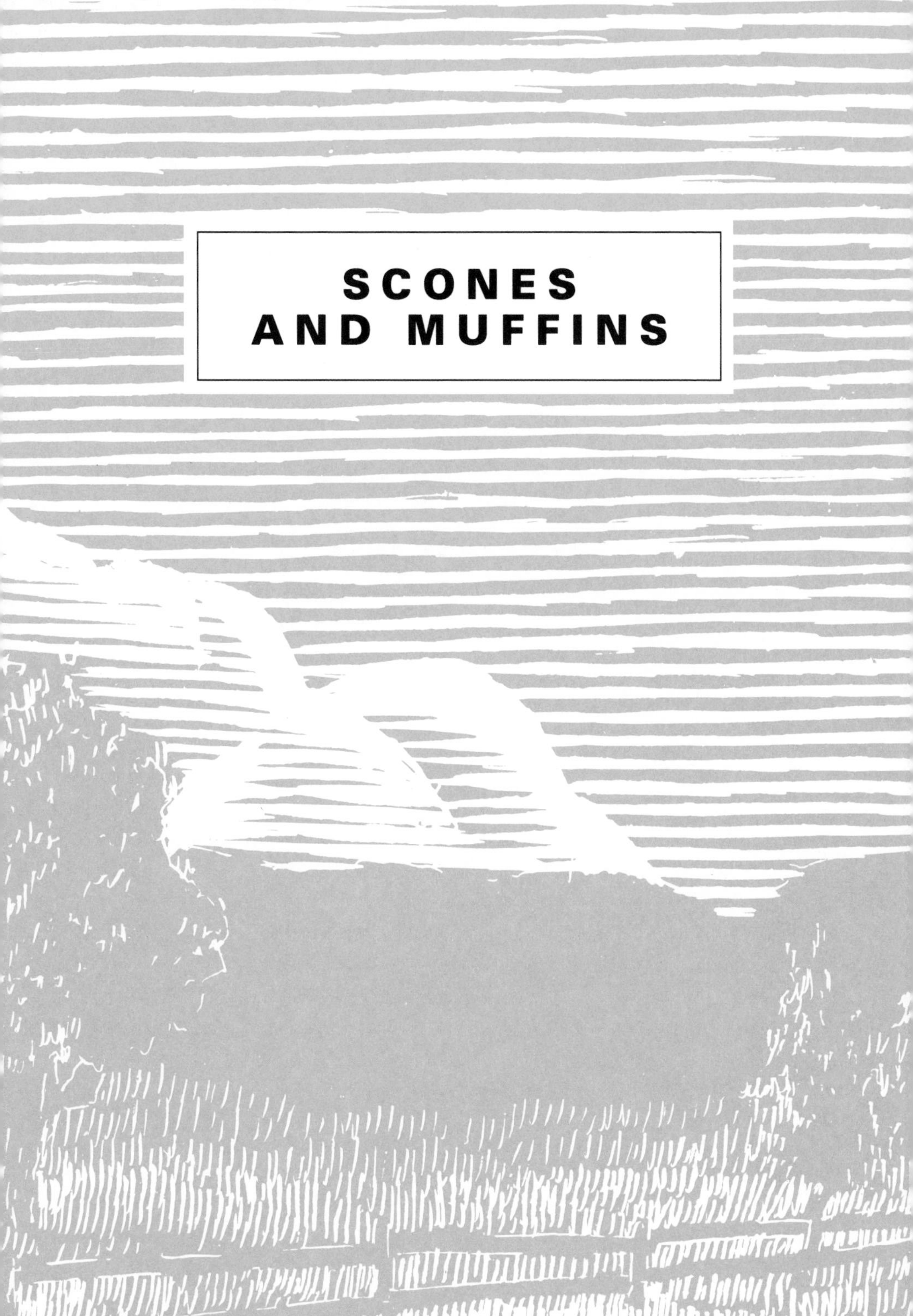

SCONES AND MUFFINS

STUFFED SCONES

THE BEECH TREE MANOR

SEATTLE, WASHINGTON

1½ cups all-purpose flour

2 teaspoons cream of tartar

2 tablespoons sugar

1 teaspoon baking soda

3 tablespoons chilled butter

½ cup milk

FILLING:

1 pint blueberries, fresh or frozen

1 tablespoon cornstarch

1 tablespoon sugar

Sliced berries in season (strawberries, raspberries, blackberries, etc.)

Whipped cream (optional)

Preheat oven to 400 degrees.

To prepare scones, in a medium bowl, combine flour, cream of tartar, sugar, and baking soda. Cut in butter until mixture is the consistency of coarse crumbs. Add milk; toss lightly until well blended. Pat into a circle ½-inch thick; cut into fourths. Place scones on a lightly greased cookie sheet. Bake for 15 minutes, until golden brown. Meanwhile, combine blueberries, cornstarch, and sugar in a medium saucepan. Cook over medium heat until blueberries form a sauce. Add other berries and heat until warm. Split scones and fill with fruit. Top with whipped cream, if desired.

FOUR SERVINGS

ORANGE SCONES

THE JAMES HOUSE

PORT TOWNSEND, WASHINGTON

2 cups all-purpose flour

2 tablespoons sugar

1 tablespoon baking powder

½ teaspoon salt

¾ cup dried currants

1 tablespoon finely grated orange rind

6 tablespoons butter

1 egg, lightly beaten

½ cup milk

Preheat oven to 400 degrees. In a large bowl, combine flour, sugar, baking powder, and salt. Stir in currants and orange rind. Cut in butter until crumbly. Add egg and milk. Stir until dough clings together. Knead gently (12 to 15 times) on a lightly floured board. Cut dough into fourths and form squares about ½ inch thick. Cut each square diagonally twice to form 4 triangles. Place squares on a lightly greased baking sheet (or freeze for future baking). Bake for 15 to 20 minutes, until golden brown.

SIXTEEN SCONES

SCOTTISH SCONES

HEATHER HOUSE

EDMONDS, WASHINGTON

2 cups sifted all-purpose flour

2 tablespoons sugar

½ teaspoon baking soda

½ teaspoon salt

¼ cup butter or margarine

½ cup raisins, soaked in warm water for 20 minutes and drained

¾ cup plus 2 tablespoons sour milk

Preheat oven to 450 degrees. Sift together flour, sugar, baking soda, and salt into a mixing bowl. Cut butter or margarine into small pieces and add to dry ingredients. Blend together until mixture is crumbly. Make a well in the center of the mixture and add raisins. Stir gently until well blended. Make another well and gradually add the sour milk, stirring lightly with a fork. Mix just until a soft dough is formed. Turn onto a lightly floured surface and divide into 3 equal parts. Pat each piece into a circle ½ inch thick at the edge, with the center slightly thicker. Cut each circle into 4 equal pieces. Place each of the 12 pieces on an ungreased baking sheet. Bake for 12 to 15 minutes, until golden brown. Best served warm.

TWELVE SCONES

FRENCH BREAKFAST PUFFS

ABIGAIL'S

VICTORIA, BRITISH COLUMBIA

⅓ cup shortening or margarine

½ cup sugar

1 egg

1½ cups all-purpose flour

1½ teaspoons baking powder

½ teaspoon salt

¼ teaspoon nutmeg

½ cup milk

½ cup butter or margarine, melted

½ cup sugar, mixed with ½ teaspoon cinnamon

Preheat oven to 350 degrees. In a large bowl, cream shortening, sugar, and egg. In a separate bowl, combine flour, baking powder, salt, and nutmeg. Add to creamed mixture alternately with milk. Fill greased muffin tins two-thirds full. Bake for 20 to 25 minutes, or until golden brown. Remove puffs from oven and immediately roll in melted butter and then in cinnamon sugar.

FIFTEEN PUFFS

RASPBERRY MUFFINS

EAGLES NEST INN

LANGLEY, WASHINGTON

1½ cups all-purpose flour

¼ cup granulated sugar

¼ cup packed brown sugar

2 teaspoons baking powder

¼ teaspoon cinnamon

1 egg, lightly beaten

½ cup milk

½ cup butter or margarine, melted

1¼ cups fresh raspberries, (if frozen, mix with 2 tablespoons flour)

TOPPING:

½ cup chopped nuts

½ cup packed brown sugar

¼ cup flour

2 teaspoons grated orange rind

1 teaspoon cinnamon

Preheat oven to 350 degrees. In a bowl, combine flour, sugars, baking powder, and cinnamon. Make a well in center and add egg, milk, and butter. Stir with a wooden spoon just until blended, being careful not to overmix. Gently fold in raspberries. Fill greased muffin tins two-thirds full. For topping, in a bowl combine nuts, brown sugar, flour, orange rind, and cinnamon. Sprinkle each muffin with 1 tablespoon of topping. Bake for 20 to 25 minutes, until muffins test done.

TWELVE MUFFINS

OATMEAL PEACH MUFFINS

GALER PLACE

SEATTLE, WASHINGTON

1¼ cups all-purpose flour

1 cup rolled oats

¼ cup packed brown sugar

1½ teaspoons cinnamon

1 teaspoon baking soda

1 teaspoon baking powder

1 cup buttermilk

½ cup vegetable oil

2 tablespoons molasses

1 egg

1 teaspoon vanilla extract

¾ cup chopped walnuts

1 cup peeled, chopped fresh peaches

Preheat oven to 400 degrees. In a large bowl, combine flour, oats, brown sugar, cinnamon, baking soda, and baking powder. In a medium bowl, combine buttermilk, oil, molasses, egg, and vanilla extract. Add wet ingredients to dry ingredients and mix just until blended. (Batter will be lumpy.) Stir in walnuts and peaches. Fill greased muffin tins two-thirds full. Bake for 20 minutes, until muffins test done.

TWELVE MUFFINS

APPLESAUCE MUFFINS

GLENACRES INN

WESTPORT, WASHINGTON

½ cup butter or margarine, softened

½ cup sugar

2 eggs

¾ cup applesauce

1¾ cups all-purpose flour

1 teaspoon baking soda

½ cup finely chopped walnuts

½ cup raisins

1 tablespoon coconut

½ teaspoon salt

Preheat oven to 400 degrees. In a large bowl, cream butter or margarine and sugar until fluffy. Beat in eggs until light. Add applesauce. In a separate bowl, stir together flour, baking soda, nuts, raisins, coconut, and salt. Add to applesauce mixture, stirring just until blended. Fill greased muffin tins two-thirds full. Bake for 15 minutes, until muffins test done.

TWELVE MUFFINS

ENGLISH TEA MUFFINS

JOSHUA GRINDLE INN

MENDOCINO, CALIFORNIA

2 cups all-purpose flour

2 teaspoons baking powder

½ teaspoon salt

½ teaspoon cinnamon

¾ cup granulated sugar

½ cup butter

1 egg

1 cup milk

¾ cup raisins

TOPPING:

½ cup packed brown sugar

¼ cup chopped nuts

1 teaspoon cinnamon

Preheat oven to 350 degrees. In a bowl, combine flour, baking powder, salt, and cinnamon. In a large bowl, cream sugar and butter. Beat in egg. Add flour mixture to creamed mixture alternately with milk. Fold in raisins. Fill greased muffin tins two-thirds full. For topping, in a bowl combine brown sugar, nuts, and cinnamon. Sprinkle each muffin with 1 tablespoon topping. Bake for 20 minutes, until muffins test done. Note: Batter will keep in refrigerator for up to 2 weeks.

TWELVE MUFFINS

LEMON-ZUCCHINI MUFFINS

KANGAROO HOUSE

EASTSOUND, WASHINGTON

1½ cups all-purpose flour

½ cup oat bran

1 tablespoon baking powder

1 teaspoon grated lemon rind

½ teaspoon salt

½ teaspoon nutmeg

½ cup chopped nuts

½ cup golden raisins

2 eggs

½ cup milk

½ cup granulated sugar

⅓ cup vegetable oil

1 cup shredded zucchini, packed

TOPPING:

3 tablespoons each flour, sugar, and wheat germ

2 tablespoons butter, softened

1 teaspoon grated lemon rind

Preheat oven to 400 degrees. In a large bowl, combine flour, oat bran, baking powder, lemon rind, salt, and nutmeg. Stir in nuts and raisins. In a small bowl, beat eggs with a fork; blend in milk, sugar, and oil. Add to flour mixture with zucchini. Stir just until blended. Fill greased muffin tins two-thirds full. For topping, in a small bowl, combine flour, sugar, wheat germ, butter, and lemon rind until crumbly. Sprinkle each muffin with 1 tablespoon of topping. Bake for 20 minutes, until muffins test done.

TWELVE MUFFINS

POPPY SEED MUFFINS

THE GALLERY AT LITTLE CAPEHORN

CATHLAMET, WASHINGTON

½ cup butter

¾ cup sugar

2 eggs

¾ cup sour cream

1½ teaspoons vanilla extract

2 cups all-purpose flour

⅓ cup poppy seed

½ teaspoon salt

¼ teaspoon baking soda

Cinnamon sugar (¼ cup sugar mixed with ¼ teaspoon cinnamon)

Preheat oven to 375 degrees. In a large bowl, cream butter and sugar. Blend in eggs, sour cream, and vanilla extract. In a separate bowl, combine flour, poppy seed, salt, and baking soda, and add to creamed mixture. Fill greased muffin tins two-thirds full. Sprinkle with cinnamon sugar. Bake for 20 minutes, until golden brown.

TWELVE MUFFINS

APRICOT MUFFINS

ROBERTA'S BED & BREAKFAST

SEATTLE, WASHINGTON

2 cups all-purpose flour

⅔ cup sugar

1 tablespoon baking powder

¼ teaspoon salt

1 egg, lightly beaten

⅓ cup butter or margarine, melted

¾ cup orange juice

½ cup milk

1 tablespoon grated orange rind

1 cup chopped nuts

1 cup chopped dried apricots

Preheat oven to 400 degrees. Sift together flour, sugar, baking powder, and salt; set aside. In a large bowl, combine egg, butter or margarine, orange juice, milk, orange rind, nuts, and apricots. Stir in flour mixture, and mix just until blended. Fill greased muffin tins two-thirds full. Bake for 20 minutes, until muffins test done.

TWELVE MUFFINS

BLUEBERRY MUFFINS

SAN JUAN INN

FRIDAY HARBOR, WASHINGTON

3 cups all-purpose flour

½ cup granulated sugar

1½ tablespoons baking powder

½ teaspoon salt

¾ cup blueberries

3 eggs

1½ cups milk

⅓ cup vegetable oil

TOPPING:

½ cup packed brown sugar

½ cup chopped walnuts

1 teaspoon cinnamon

Preheat oven to 400 degrees. In a large bowl, combine flour, sugar, baking powder, and salt. Stir in blueberries. In a separate bowl, beat eggs; add milk and oil. Stir well and add to dry mixture. Fold gently just until moistened. Fill greased muffin tins two-thirds full. For topping, in a small bowl combine brown sugar, walnuts, and cinnamon. Sprinkle each muffin with 1 tablespoon of topping. Bake for 20 minutes, until muffins test done.

TWELVE MUFFINS

ORANGE YOGURT MUFFINS

TOP O' TRIANGLE MOUNTAIN

VICTORIA, BRITISH COLUMBIA

1 cup all-purpose flour (use half whole wheat if desired)

1 cup wheat germ

4 teaspoons baking powder

½ teaspoon salt

¼ teaspoon baking soda

2 tablespoons butter

1 cup packed brown sugar

1 egg

1 teaspoon grated orange rind

¼ cup orange juice

¾ cup plain yogurt

Preheat oven to 425 degrees. In a medium bowl, combine flour, wheat germ, baking powder, salt, and baking soda. In a large bowl, cream together butter, brown sugar, and egg; add orange rind, juice, and yogurt. Mix in dry ingredients and stir just until blended. Fill greased muffin tins two-thirds full. Bake for 15 to 18 minutes, until muffins test done.

TWELVE MUFFINS

BANANA–OAT BRAN MUFFINS

LAKE CHELAN RIVER HOUSE

CHELAN, WASHINGTON

1 egg

¾ cup packed light brown sugar

3 ripe bananas, mashed (1⅓ cups)

1 cup raisins or walnuts

⅓ cup vegetable oil

1 teaspoon vanilla extract

¼ cup molasses

½ cup coconut

¾ cup all-purpose flour

¾ cup whole wheat flour

½ cup oat bran

2 teaspoons baking powder

½ teaspoon baking soda

1 teaspoon cinnamon

¼ teaspoon salt

Preheat oven to 375 degrees. In a medium bowl, whisk together egg and sugar. Beat in bananas, raisins, oil, vanilla extract, molasses, and coconut. In a separate bowl, combine flours, oat bran, baking powder, baking soda, cinnamon, and salt. Using a spatula, gently fold in banana mixture and stir just until blended. Fill greased muffin tins two-thirds full. Bake for 20 minutes, until golden brown. Turn out onto a cooling rack to cool.

TWELVE MUFFINS

WHOLESOME BRAN MUFFINS

COLONEL CROCKETT FARM
BED & BREAKFAST INN

COUPEVILLE, WASHINGTON

2 cups Bran Buds cereal

1¼ cups all-purpose flour

1 cup whole wheat flour

1¼ teaspoons baking soda

1 teaspoon cinnamon

½ teaspoon nutmeg

½ teaspoon salt

2 tablespoons honey

2 cups buttermilk

1 egg

½ cup dark molasses

2 tablespoons vegetable oil

1 cup grated carrot

½ cup raisins

½ cup chopped walnuts

Preheat oven to 350 degrees. In a large bowl, combine cereal, flours, baking soda, cinnamon, nutmeg, and salt. In a separate bowl, beat honey, buttermilk, egg, molasses, and oil; add to flour mixture. Stir in carrot, raisins, and walnuts until well blended. (Batter will be thin). Fill greased muffin tins two-thirds full. Bake for 20 to 25 minutes, until muffins test done.

TWO DOZEN MUFFINS

COFFEE CAKES AND COBBLERS

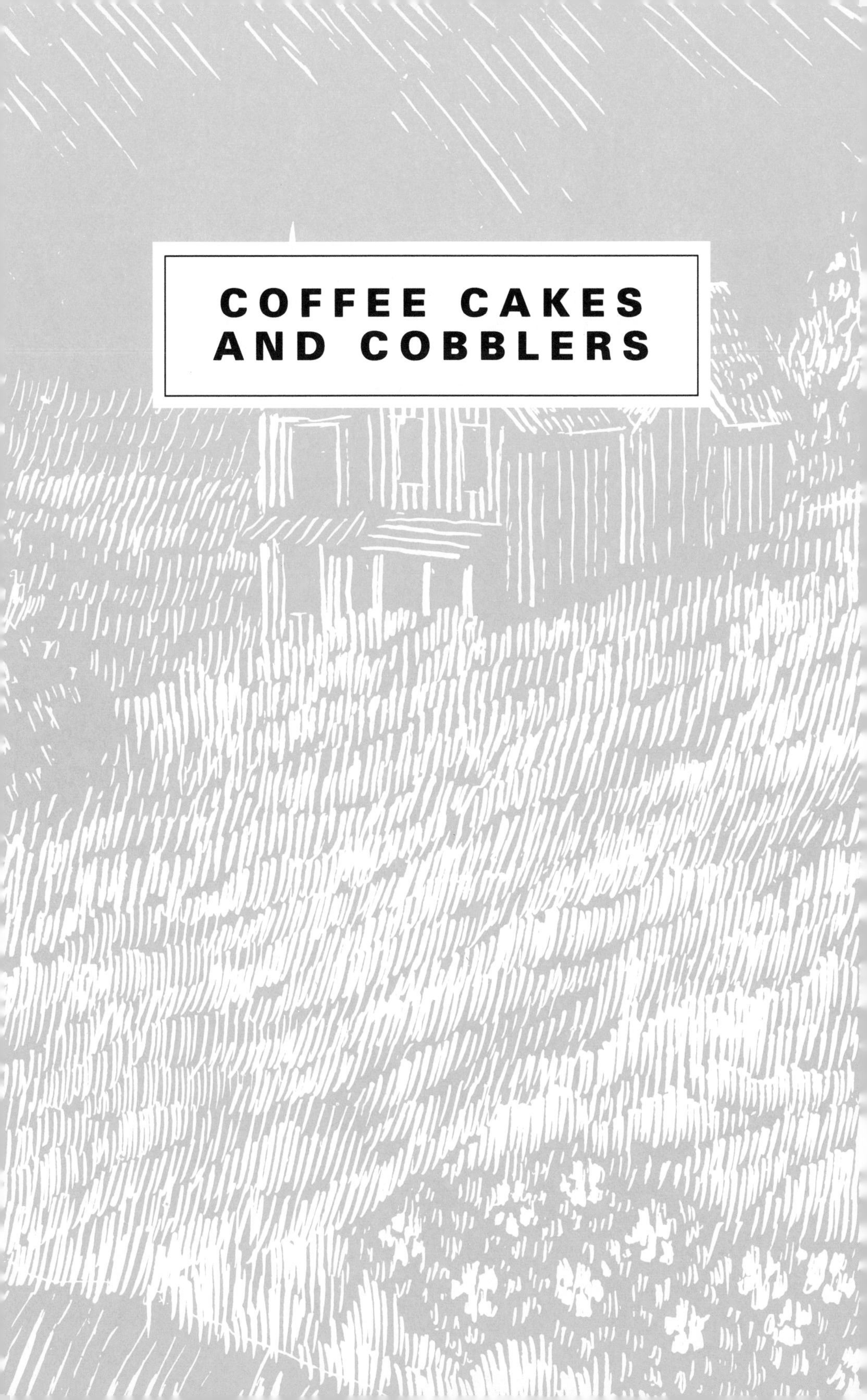

ALMOND–SOUR CREAM COFFEE CAKE

GROWLY BEAR BED & BREAKFAST

ASHFORD, WASHINGTON

½ cup butter or margarine

⅔ cup packed brown sugar

2 cups all-purpose flour

1 cup sour cream

2 eggs

1 teaspoon baking powder

1 teaspoon baking soda

1 teaspoon almond extract

TOPPING:

½ cup chopped almonds

½ cup packed brown sugar

1 teaspoon cinnamon

Preheat oven to 350 degrees. For topping, in a small bowl, combine almonds, brown sugar, and cinnamon; set aside. In a large bowl, cream butter and brown sugar until light and fluffy. Lightly beat in flour, sour cream, eggs, baking powder, baking soda, and almond extract; beat until fluffy. Spread half the batter into a greased 10-inch springform pan. Sprinkle with half the topping. Spoon dollops of the remaining batter on top and spread evenly with a spatula. Sprinkle with remaining topping. Bake for 25 to 30 minutes, until cake tests done. Cool completely in pan before cutting.

TWELVE SERVINGS

FRESH APPLE COFFEE CAKE

PINKHAM'S PILLOW

EDMONDS, WASHINGTON

1 cup all-purpose flour

½ teaspoon baking soda

2 cups peeled, cored, diced apple

1 egg

¼ cup vegetable oil

1 cup sugar

1 teaspoon cinnamon

¼ teaspoon nutmeg

½ cup chopped nuts

Preheat oven to 350 degrees. In a small bowl, sift together flour and baking soda; set aside. Place apples in a medium bowl. Break egg over apples. Add oil, sugar, spices, and nuts; mix well. Add flour mixture to apple mixture and stir just until blended. (Batter will be slightly dry.) Spread batter into a greased 8-inch-square baking pan. Bake for 40 to 45 minutes, until golden brown. Let cool 10 minutes before cutting.

EIGHT SERVINGS

BANANA-ALMOND COFFEE CAKE

PENSION EDELWEISS

WHISTLER, BRITISH COLUMBIA

6 tablespoons butter

¾ cup sugar

2 eggs, lightly beaten

1¼ cups all-purpose flour

½ teaspoon baking powder

½ cup milk

2 or 3 bananas

Juice of half a lemon

½ cup sliced almonds

Confectioners' sugar

Preheat oven to 400 degrees. In a medium bowl, cream butter and sugar until light and fluffy; add eggs. In a separate bowl, combine flour and baking powder; add to butter mixture alternately with milk. Pour half of batter into a greased 5- by 9-inch loaf pan. Cut bananas lengthwise and sprinkle with lemon juice. Lay bananas on top of batter and sprinkle with ¼ cup almonds. (Bananas will sink slightly.) Pour remaining batter over bananas and sprinkle with remaining almonds. Bake for 50–55 minutes, until cake tests done. Cool. Dust with confectioners' sugar.

EIGHT SERVINGS

BLUEBERRY COFFEE CAKE

AMY'S MANOR BED & BREAKFAST

PATEROS, WASHINGTON

2 cups all-purpose flour

¾ cup sugar

2½ teaspoons baking powder

½ teaspoon salt

¼ cup butter or margarine

¾ cup milk

1 egg

2 cups fresh or frozen blueberries (thawed and drained, if frozen)

TOPPING:

½ cup sugar

⅓ cup all-purpose flour

½ teaspoon cinnamon

¼ teaspoon nutmeg

¼ cup butter, softened

Preheat oven to 375 degrees. In a bowl, blend together flour, sugar, baking powder, salt, butter or margarine, milk, and egg. Using an electric mixer, beat vigorously for 30 seconds. Carefully stir blueberries into batter. Pour into a greased 9-inch-square cake pan. For topping, in a bowl combine sugar, flour, cinnamon, nutmeg, and butter; sprinkle over batter. Bake for 45 to 50 minutes, until cake tests done.

NINE SERVINGS

COFFEE CAKE SUPREME

THE HOPE-MERRILL, HOPE-BOSWORTH HOUSE

GEYSERVILLE, CALIFORNIA

½ cup butter

½ cup sugar

½ teaspoon vanilla extract

1 egg

1½ cups all-purpose flour

1½ teaspoons baking powder

½ teaspoon salt

½ cup milk

¼ cup chopped walnuts

FILLING:

¼ cup butter, melted

½ cup packed brown sugar

1 tablespoon all-purpose flour

1 tablespoon cinnamon

¼ cup chopped walnuts

¼ cup chopped dates

Preheat oven to 350 degrees. In a medium bowl, thoroughly cream butter, sugar, and vanilla extract. Beat in egg. Sift together flour, baking powder, and salt, and add to creamed mixture alternately with milk. Spread half the batter in a greased 8-inch-square cake pan. For filling, in a separate bowl, combine butter, brown sugar, flour, cinnamon, walnuts, and dates; sprinkle over batter. Spread remaining batter over filling. Top with nuts. Bake for 45 minutes, until cake tests done.

EIGHT SERVINGS

CREAM CHEESE COFFEE CAKE

THE ESTATE INN

GUERNEVILLE, CALIFORNIA

2¼ cups all-purpose flour

1 cup sugar

¾ cup butter

1 teaspoon cinnamon

½ teaspoon baking powder

½ teaspoon baking soda

¼ teaspoon salt

¾ cup sour cream

2 eggs

1 teaspoon almond extract

8 ounces cream cheese, softened

1 cup apple-cinnamon jelly, or another flavor of jam or jelly

½ cup slivered almonds

Preheat oven to 350 degrees. Grease and flour a 10-inch spring-form pan. In a bowl, combine flour and ¾ cup of the sugar; cut in butter until mixture resembles coarse crumbs. Reserve 1 cup of this mixture. To the remaining crumb mixture, add cinnamon, baking powder, baking soda, salt, sour cream, 1 of the eggs, and almond extract; blend well. Spread carefully over the bottom and about 2 inches up the sides of the spring-form pan. In a bowl, combine cream cheese, the remaining ¼ cup sugar, and the remaining egg, and blend well. Spread cream cheese mixture over the batter in the pan. Spoon apple-cinnamon jelly over cream cheese filling. Spread the reserved crumb mixture on top of the jelly layer. Sprinkle with slivered almonds. Bake for 1 hour, until filling is set and crust is golden brown. Cool for 15 minutes before removing the sides of the pan.

SIXTEEN SERVINGS

GRAHAM CRACKER CRUMBCAKE

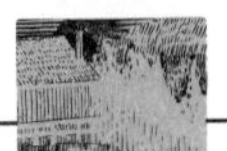

THE WILLIAMS HOUSE

SEATTLE, WASHINGTON

½ cup butter or margarine

⅔ cup granulated sugar

⅔ cup packed brown sugar

3 eggs

1 teaspoon vanilla extract

½ cup all-purpose flour

1½ cups graham cracker crumbs

1 teaspoon baking powder

½ teaspoon salt

1 cup buttermilk

1 cup chopped walnuts

Preheat oven to 350 degrees. In a large bowl, cream butter and sugars; stir in eggs and vanilla extract. In a medium bowl, combine flour, graham cracker crumbs, baking powder, and salt, and add to butter mixture alternately with buttermilk. Fold in nuts. Pour into a greased 9-inch-square cake pan. Bake for 40 minutes, until cake tests done.

NINE SERVINGS

RHUBARB–SOUR CREAM COFFEE CAKE

CHANTICLEER INN

ASHLAND, OREGON

¼ cup butter, softened

1½ cups light brown sugar, packed

1 egg

1 teaspoon vanilla extract

2⅓ cups all-purpose flour

1 teaspoon baking soda

4 cups chopped rhubarb

1 cup sour cream

Freshly grated nutmeg

Whipped cream (optional)

Preheat oven to 350 degrees. In a large bowl, cream butter and sugar until fluffy; beat in egg and vanilla extract. Combine flour and baking soda; add to butter mixture. Stir in rhubarb and sour cream. Mix dough with hands, as this is a very stiff batter. Pat into a greased 9- by 13-inch baking dish. Sprinkle lightly with nutmeg. Bake for 40 minutes, until cake tests done. Serve warm, topped with whipped cream, if desired.

TWELVE SERVINGS

STICKY BREAD COFFEE CAKE

TUCKER'S BED & BREAKFAST

VICTORIA, BRITISH COLUMBIA

1 cup packed brown sugar

1 egg

¼ cup water

1 teaspoon baking soda

1 teaspoon cinnamon

⅛ teaspoon crushed whole cloves

½ cup raisins

1 loaf frozen bread dough, thawed

Preheat oven to 350 degrees. In a large bowl, combine brown sugar, egg, water, baking soda, cinnamon, and cloves. Stir in raisins. Tear bread dough into 1-inch cubes and toss with brown sugar mixture. Place in a greased 9-inch-square cake pan. Bake for 25 to 30 minutes, until lightly browned.

NINE SERVINGS

YOGURT COCONUT COFFEE CAKE

VICTORIANA BED & BREAKFAST

SEASIDE, OREGON

½ cup butter

½ cup shortening

1 cup granulated sugar

2 eggs

2 cups all-purpose flour

1 teaspoon baking soda

½ teaspoon salt

1 cup yogurt

1 teaspoon vanilla extract

TOPPING:

⅓ cup granulated sugar

⅓ cup packed brown sugar

1 teaspoon cinnamon

½ cup coconut

Preheat oven to 350 degrees. In a large bowl, cream butter, shortening, and sugar; beat in eggs. Sift together flour, baking soda, and salt; add to butter mixture. Stir in yogurt and vanilla extract; mix well. For topping, in a small bowl, combine sugars, cinnamon, and coconut. Pour half of the batter into a greased and floured 9- by 13-inch baking dish. Sprinkle with half of the topping. Pour remaining batter on top and sprinkle with remaining topping. Bake for 30 minutes, until cake tests done.

TWELVE SERVINGS

APPLE–OAT BRAN CRUMBLE

WHITE SWAN GUEST HOUSE

MOUNT VERNON, WASHINGTON

6 tart apples, peeled, cored, and chopped

2 tablespoons lemon juice

½ cup golden raisins

¾ cup packed brown sugar

½ cup quick-cooking oatmeal

⅓ cup all-purpose flour

⅓ cup oat bran

¾ cup butter

1 tablespoon cinnamon

Vanilla yogurt (optional)

Preheat oven to 375 degrees. In a large bowl, combine apples and lemon juice; stir in raisins. Place in a greased 8- by 12-inch baking dish. In a bowl, combine sugar, oatmeal, flour, oat bran, butter, and cinnamon; mix until crumbly. Spread mixture over apples. Bake for 30 minutes, until apples are tender. Serve warm with a dollop of yogurt, if desired.

EIGHT SERVINGS

BLUEBERRY SOURDOUGH COBBLER

CHAMBERED NAUTILUS

SEATTLE, WASHINGTON

5 to 6 slices sourdough bread

4 eggs

½ cup milk

¼ teaspoon baking powder

1 teaspoon vanilla extract

½ cup sugar

1½ teaspoons cornstarch

1 teaspoon cinnamon

¼ teaspoon nutmeg

6 cups fresh blueberries or 28 ounces frozen blueberries (do not thaw)

3 tablespoons butter, melted

Trim crusts from bread and slice into 1- or 1½-inch fingers. Place on a rimmed cookie sheet. In a bowl, beat together eggs, milk, baking powder, and vanilla extract. Pour over bread until thoroughly covered. Cover with plastic wrap and refrigerate overnight.

Next day, preheat oven to 450 degrees. In a large bowl, combine sugar, cornstarch, cinnamon, and nutmeg. Stir in blueberries. Spread berries in a greased 9- by 13-inch baking dish. Carefully lift bread and place it soaked side up on top of berries, wedging pieces together to make a solid "crust." Drizzle melted butter over top of bread. Bake for 25 minutes until crisp and lightly browned. Let stand 5 minutes before serving. Cut into squares and lift carefully onto plates, spooning juice and berries over top.

EIGHT SERVINGS

"BLUEBARB" CRUNCH

SCHNAUZER CROSSING

BELLINGHAM, WASHINGTON

4 cups rhubarb, in 1-inch pieces

2 cups blueberries

1 cup granulated sugar

½ cup all-purpose flour

1 teaspoon cinnamon

1 teaspoon lemon juice

½ cup water

TOPPING:

1 cup all-purpose flour

1 cup packed brown sugar

½ cup rolled oats

½ cup butter or margarine, melted

½ cup chopped walnuts (optional)

Preheat oven to 375 degrees. In a large bowl, combine rhubarb, blueberries, sugar, flour, cinnamon, lemon juice, and water; mix well. Pour into a greased 9- by 12-inch baking dish. For topping, in a small bowl, combine flour, brown sugar, oats, butter or margarine, and walnuts, if desired. Sprinkle topping over fruit. Bake for 45 minutes, until rhubarb is tender. Best served warm.

EIGHT SERVINGS

BLACKBERRY COBBLER

SYLVAN HAUS

MONTESANO, WASHINGTON

1½ cups fresh blackberries

½ cup sugar

2 teaspoons cornstarch

CRUST:

1 cup all-purpose flour

1½ teaspoons baking powder

3 teaspoons sugar

¼ teaspoon salt

¼ cup shortening or margarine

⅓ cup milk

Granola, yogurt, cream, or whipped topping (optional)

Preheat oven to 450 degrees. Rinse and drain berries. In a medium bowl, combine sugar and cornstarch; mix with berries. For crust, sift flour 3 times and combine with baking powder, sugar, and salt. Cut in shortening until mixture resembles coarse crumbs. Add milk and knead dough 6 to 8 times. On a floured board, roll out dough into a 12-inch circle. Place in an 8-inch pie pan. (Dough will hang over edge of pan.) Fill pie shell with berries. Fold excess dough toward center, leaving middle open. Bake for 10 minutes, reduce heat to 325 degrees, and bake 20 minutes longer, until crust is brown. Serve in small bowls with granola, yogurt, cream, or whipped topping, if desired.

SIX SERVINGS

RASPBERRY KUCHEN

BELLE DE JOUR INN

HEALDSBURG, CALIFORNIA

1 egg, well beaten

½ cup sugar

½ cup milk

2 tablespoons vegetable oil

1 cup all-purpose flour

2 teaspoons baking powder

1 cup fresh raspberries

TOPPING:

½ cup all-purpose flour

½ cup sugar

3 tablespoons butter

Preheat oven to 375 degrees. In a bowl, combine egg, sugar, milk, and oil; mix well. Sift together flour and baking powder; stir into egg mixture. Pour into a greased 8-inch-square cake pan. Sprinkle raspberries over batter. For topping, in a small bowl, mix flour with sugar. Cut in butter until mixture resembles coarse crumbs. Sprinkle topping over raspberries. Bake for 25 to 30 minutes, until cake tests done. Best served warm.

SIXTEEN SQUARES

HOUSE SPECIALTIES

EASY STICKY BUNS

THE BED & BREAKFAST INN

SAN FRANCISCO, CALIFORNIA

½ cup pecans

½ cup butter

1 cup packed light brown sugar

2 tablespoons water

2 tubes (8 oz. each) crescent dinner rolls

½ cup raisins

1 teaspoon cinnamon

Preheat oven to 350 degrees. Sprinkle ¼ cup of the pecans in the bottom of a greased bundt pan. In a small saucepan, combine butter, brown sugar, water, and the remaining ¼ cup pecans. Bring mixture to a boil and simmer 1 minute. Pour half of the brown sugar mixture over the pecans in the pan. Slice each roll of crescent dough into 8 pieces. Arrange the contents of one tube of rolls, cut side up, over the brown sugar mixture in the pan. Sprinkle with ¼ cup of the raisins and ½ teaspoon of the cinnamon. Spoon remaining brown sugar mixture over the raisins and cinnamon. Place remaining dough slices on top, overlapping the lower slices. Sprinkle the remaining ¼ cup raisins and ½ teaspoon cinnamon over the dough. Bake for 25 minutes, until golden brown. Cool on a rack for 10 minutes, and then invert the pan to unmold the buns.

SIXTEEN SERVINGS

BREAKFAST PRETZELS

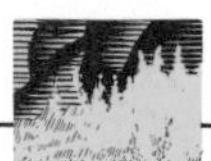

THE CLINKERBRICK HOUSE

PORTLAND, OREGON

1 package active dry yeast

1 teaspoon salt

1 tablespoon sugar

1½ cups water, heated to 115 degrees

4 cups all-purpose flour

½ cup dried currants or raisins

1 teaspoon cinnamon

1 egg, beaten

Cinnamon sugar (¼ cup sugar mixed with ¼ teaspoon cinnamon)

Cream cheese (optional)

Preheat oven to 425 degrees. In a small bowl, dissolve yeast, salt, and sugar in the warm water. In a large bowl or food processor, combine flour, currants, cinnamon, and yeast mixture; mix well. Process or knead until dough is smooth and elastic. Divide into 12 pieces. Roll each piece into a rope and twist into a pretzel shape. Place on a greased cookie sheet. Brush with egg and sprinkle with cinnamon-sugar mixture. Bake for 10 to 12 minutes, until golden brown. Serve warm with cream cheese, if desired.

TWELVE PRETZELS

SWISS MUESLI

CHALET LUISE

WHISTLER, BRITISH COLUMBIA

1 cup rolled oats

1 cup orange juice

Juice of half a lemon

¼ cup raisins

¼ cup chopped nuts

3 cups chopped fresh fruit

1 cup plain yogurt

Dash cinnamon

Sugar to taste

Whipped cream (optional)

In a large bowl, combine oats, orange juice, and lemon juice. Mix in raisins, nuts, and fresh fruit. Stir in yogurt. Add cinnamon and sugar to taste. Fold in whipped cream, or top with dollops of whipped cream, and additional fruit, if desired.

FOUR SERVINGS

BIRCHER MUESLI

MOLE HOUSE

MERCER ISLAND, WASHINGTON

1½ cups rolled oats

2½ cups milk

1½ tablespoons lemon juice

2 small apples, diced

¼ cup packed brown sugar

¼ cup finely chopped hazelnuts

Raisins and cinnamon (optional)

In a large bowl, combine oats and milk; let stand 15 minutes. Sprinkle lemon juice over apples; drain. Before serving, stir apples and brown sugar into oat mixture. Spoon into individual serving bowls and sprinkle with nuts and with raisins and cinnamon, if desired.

FOUR SERVINGS

HONEY GRANOLA

DOWNEY HOUSE BED & BREAKFAST

LA CONNER, WASHINGTON

5 cups old-fashioned rolled oats (not quick-cooking)

1 cup coconut

1 cup wheat germ

1 cup chopped raw almonds

½ cup sesame seed

½ cup sunflower seed

½ teaspoon salt

½ cup honey

1 cup corn oil

2 teaspoons vanilla extract

Preheat oven to 300 degrees. In a large bowl, combine oats, coconut, wheat germ, almonds, sesame seed, and sunflower seed; set aside. In a small saucepan, warm honey with oil and vanilla extract over medium heat. Add to dry ingredients and mix thoroughly. Spread mixture evenly in a greased 10- by 15-inch jelly-roll pan. Bake for 40 to 45 minutes, stirring every 10 minutes, until cereal is lightly browned. Store in an airtight container.

9 CUPS

SUPER STARTER OATMEAL

SCARLETT'S COUNTRY INN

CALISTOGA, CALIFORNIA

2 cups old-fashioned rolled oats (not quick-cooking)

4 cups low-fat milk

¼ teaspoon salt

1 fresh ripe nectarine, peeled and chopped

1 apple, peeled, cored, and chopped

1 banana, peeled and chopped

¼ cup raisins

In a medium saucepan, combine oats, milk, salt, fruit, and raisins; let soak for several minutes. Simmer slowly over low heat, stirring frequently. Cook until mixture becomes thickened, about 10 minutes. Serve warm in individual serving bowls.

SIX SERVINGS

MORNING PIE

THE BLAIR HOUSE

BED & BREAKFAST INN

FRIDAY HARBOR, WASHINGTON

2 cups cottage cheese

3 eggs

⅔ cup sugar

2 tablespoons all-purpose flour

1 teaspoon grated orange rind

1 tablespoon orange juice

¼ teaspoon orange extract

9-inch deep-dish pie shell, thawed if frozen

Preheat oven to 350 degrees. In a large bowl, beat cottage cheese with an electric mixer on high speed for 1 minute. Add eggs, sugar, flour, orange rind, orange juice, and orange extract; blend well. Pour into pie shell and bake for 50 minutes, until a knife inserted comes out clean. Refrigerate overnight; serve chilled the next morning.

SIX SERVINGS

AUSTRIAN APPLE STRUDEL

CHALET DE FRANCE

EUREKA, CALIFORNIA

1 sheet frozen prepared puff pastry

2 tablespoons butter

1 large green apple, peeled, cored, and chopped into ½-inch pieces

⅓ cup golden raisins

10 dried apricot halves, cut into quarters

⅓ cup chopped walnuts

¼ cup water

¼ cup packed light brown sugar

½ teaspoon cinnamon

¼ teaspoon nutmeg

1 egg yolk beaten with 1 tablespoon water

Remove puff pastry from freezer and thaw for 20 minutes. In a large skillet, melt butter over medium heat. Add apple, raisins, apricots, and walnuts. Mix well and sauté for a few minutes. Add water, sugar, cinnamon, and nutmeg. Cover and simmer for 10 minutes, until apples are tender but not mushy. Remove from skillet; set aside to cool. Place pastry on a flat surface and distribute apple mixture down middle. Make 2-inch cuts diagonally along both sides of pastry at 1-inch intervals. Fold strips over apples, alternating from left to right. Press dough together where ends overlap.

Seal top and bottom edges of dough with the tines of a fork. Refrigerate for 30 minutes, or freeze for later use.

Preheat oven to 425 degrees. Place strudel on a cookie sheet covered with parchment paper. Brush top with egg wash and bake for 25 minutes, until strudel is light golden brown and pastry is puffed.

SIX SERVINGS

OSLO KRINGLE

DECANN HOUSE

BELLINGHAM, WASHINGTON

1 cup water

¼ cup butter or margarine

1 cup all-purpose flour

4 eggs

¼ teaspoon almond extract

Dash salt

ICING:

1½ cups confectioners' sugar

2 tablespoons water

¼ teaspoon almond extract

Chopped nuts or coconut (optional)

Preheat oven to 425 degrees. In a medium saucepan, bring water and butter or margarine to a boil; remove from heat. Add flour and stir quickly until a ball forms. Add eggs, one at a time, mixing well after each. Add almond extract and salt; beat until shiny and well blended. Spread dough onto a greased cookie sheet and shape into a circle approximately 10 inches in diameter. Bake for 30 minutes, until light golden brown, being careful not to overbake. To make icing, place confectioners' sugar in a medium bowl and add water and almond extract; stir vigorously until smooth. Drizzle over warm kringle. Sprinkle with nuts or coconut, if desired. Serve immediately; kringle falls soon after it is removed from the oven.

FOUR SERVINGS

OLD-FASHIONED BREAD PUDDING

GRANDMÈRE'S INN

NEVADA CITY, CALIFORNIA

3 eggs, slightly beaten

½ cup sugar

Dash salt

1 teaspoon cinnamon

2 cups milk

¼ cup butter, melted

4 cups ½-inch cubes bread, coffee cake, croissants, muffins, etc.

½ cup raisins

Preheat oven to 350 degrees. In a large bowl, combine eggs, sugar, salt, cinnamon, milk, butter, bread cubes, and raisins. Pour into a greased 8-inch round baking dish. Set dish into a larger pan filled with ½ inch of hot water. Bake for 45 to 55 minutes, until golden brown.

EIGHT SERVINGS

BAKED CHEESE BLINTZ

COWSLIP'S BELLE BED & BREAKFAST

ASHLAND, OREGON

FILLING:

8 ounces cream cheese

15 ounces ricotta cheese

2 egg yolks

1 tablespoon sugar

1 teaspoon vanilla extract

BLINTZ:

½ cup butter, softened

⅓ cup sugar

6 eggs

1 cup all-purpose flour

2 teaspoons baking powder

1½ cups plain yogurt

½ cup orange juice

TOPPING:

Sweetened fruit

Preheat oven to 350 degrees. For filling, in a small bowl, beat cream cheese until smooth. Add ricotta cheese, egg yolks, sugar, and vanilla extract; mix thoroughly. Set aside. For blintz, in a large bowl, cream together butter and sugar. Add eggs and beat well. In two separate bowls, combine flour with baking powder and yogurt with orange juice. Add alternately to egg mixture, and stir until thoroughly blended. Pour half of batter into a greased 9- by 13-inch glass baking dish. Cover batter with filling, spreading evenly to sides of pan. Top with remaining batter. Bake for 50 minutes, until golden brown. Serve with sweetened fruit topping.

EIGHT SERVINGS

FINNISH OVEN PANCAKE

FRAMPTON HOUSE BED & BREAKFAST

HEALDSBURG, CALIFORNIA

½ cup butter or margarine

5 eggs

1 tablespoon sugar

1 teaspoon salt (optional)

2 cups milk

1 cup all-purpose flour

1 cup small-curd cottage cheese

1 teaspoon baking powder

Fresh berries and confectioners' sugar (optional)

Preheat oven to 425 degrees. Cut butter into small pieces and place in a 10-inch cast-iron skillet or a 9- by 13-inch glass baking dish. Heat in oven until butter is melted. Combine eggs, sugar, and salt, if desired, in blender or electric mixer; mix at high speed for 1 minute. Continue to mix while slowly adding milk, then flour, then cottage cheese, then baking powder. Pour blended mixture into hot skillet or baking dish. Bake for 35 minutes, until pancake is puffed and beginning to brown. Remove from oven. Let sit 5 to 8 minutes before cutting. (Center will fall.) Serve with fresh berries and confectioners' sugar or with butter and warm maple syrup.

SIX SERVINGS

APPLE PAN PUFF

SILVER BAY INN

STEHEKIN, WASHINGTON

2 Granny Smith apples, peeled, cored, and thinly sliced

¼ cup butter

3 eggs

½ cup all-purpose flour

½ cup milk

1 teaspoon vanilla or almond extract

Dash salt

Preheat oven to 450 degrees. Sauté apples in butter until soft. Spread apples evenly over the bottom of a glass or ceramic pie plate. In a medium bowl, beat eggs. Add flour and beat until smooth. Stir in milk, extract, and salt; pour over apples. Bake for 20 minutes, until lightly browned. Serve immediately.

FOUR SERVINGS

PUFF PANCAKE WITH BLUEBERRIES

WEST SHORE FARM BED & BREAKFAST

LUMMI ISLAND, WASHINGTON

¼ cup butter

1 cup all-purpose flour

1 cup whipping cream

2 tablespoons cornmeal

1 tablespoon baking powder

¼ teaspoon salt

4 eggs

BLUEBERRY SAUCE:

2 to 4 cups blueberries

Sugar to taste

Preheat oven to 375 degrees. Place butter in a 10-inch cast-iron skillet; set in oven for 6 to 7 minutes, or until sizzling. Meanwhile, in a large bowl, mix flour, cream, cornmeal, baking powder, salt, and eggs, and mix just until blended. Pour into hot skillet and bake for 20 to 25 minutes, until puffed and golden brown. For sauce, in a saucepan, heat blueberries and sugar over medium heat until sugar is dissolved and juice forms. Cut pancake into quarters and serve with warm Blueberry Sauce.

FOUR SERVINGS

BAKED POTATO LATKES (PANCAKES)

WHARFSIDE BED & BREAKFAST

FRIDAY HARBOR, WASHINGTON

1 medium potato

3 tablespoons vegetable oil

1 tablespoon grated onion

Salt to taste

⅛ teaspoon garlic powder

1 egg, separated

Applesauce and sour cream (optional)

Preheat oven to 450 degrees. Peel and grate potato into a bowl of cold water; let stand ½ hour or longer. Grease a 9- by 12-inch baking pan with the vegetable oil; preheat in oven for 10 minutes. Drain potatoes and squeeze out excess water. In a bowl, combine potato with onion, salt, garlic powder, and egg yolk; mix well. In a separate bowl, beat egg white until very stiff. Drain excess liquid from potato mixture. Fold egg white into potato mixture. Spoon mixture into hot pan, forming 4 patties. Bake for 8 minutes, then flip patties and bake for another 5 minutes. Latkes should be golden brown. Serve with warm applesauce and sour cream, if desired.

TWO SERVINGS

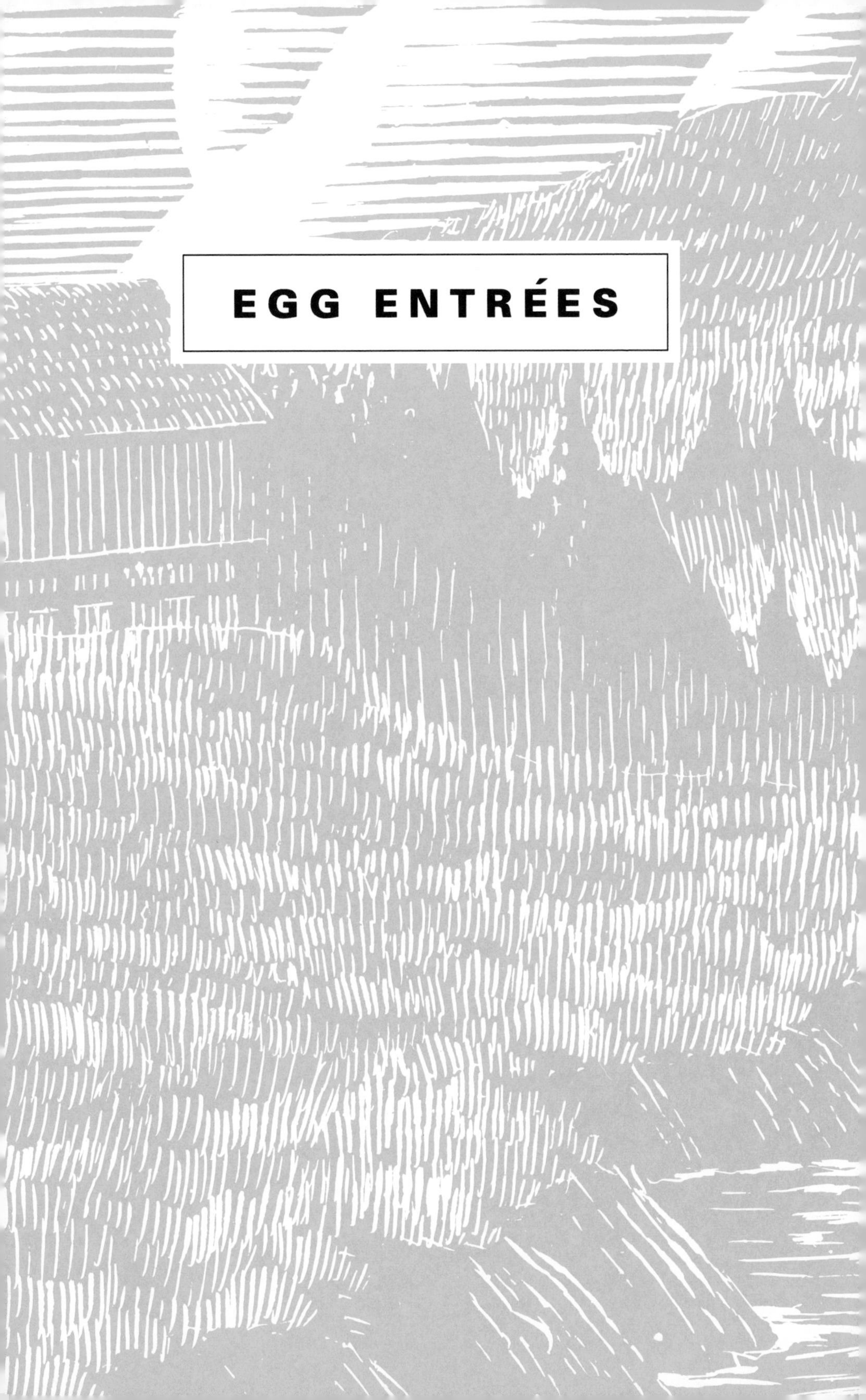

EGG ENTRÉES

ANGEL EGGS

BOMBAY HOUSE

BAINBRIDGE ISLAND, WASHINGTON

2 tablespoons sesame seed oil (not Chinese sesame oil)

2 cups angel hair pasta, cooked and drained

1½ cups diced tomato

1 cup chopped onion

½ cup minced Anaheim green chiles

¼ teaspoon pepper

⅛ teaspoon salt

4 eggs, lightly beaten

½ cup half-and-half

½ cup shredded Monterey jack cheese

½ cup shredded Gruyère cheese

Sour cream, salsa (optional)

In a large skillet, heat oil. Add the pasta and toss until heated through and slightly brown. Add tomato, onion, green chiles, pepper, and salt; toss and sauté for 2 minutes. In a medium bowl, combine eggs and half-and-half. Pour egg mixture over pasta and cook over medium heat for 5 minutes, without stirring. Sprinkle cheese over eggs. Cover pan and reduce heat. Cook 5 minutes or longer, until eggs are set. Remove from heat; cut into wedges. Serve immediately with sour cream and salsa, if desired.

SIX SERVINGS

DIVINE FILLED CROISSANTS

GROUSE MOUNTAIN BED & BREAKFAST

NORTH VANCOUVER, BRITISH COLUMBIA

4 large croissants

4 tablespoons butter

8 eggs

¼ cup milk

1 tablespoon minced fresh dill, or 1 teaspoon dried

½ cup finely chopped mushrooms

⅓ cup finely chopped smoked salmon

½ cup shredded Monterey jack cheese

Preheat oven to 225 degrees. Warm croissants in oven for 5 to 10 minutes. Meanwhile, melt butter in a medium skillet. In a bowl, beat eggs and milk together; add dill, mushrooms, and salmon. Pour into skillet and scramble until creamy. Preheat broiler. Remove croissants from oven and slice lengthwise about three-fourths of the way through (like a clamshell). Fill the croissants with the scrambled egg mixture and sprinkle with cheese. Broil croissants open-face, just until cheese is melted. Serve immediately.

FOUR SERVINGS

SCRAMBLED EGGS WITH SMOKED SALMON

MATTEY HOUSE

McMINNVILLE, OREGON

2 tablespoons butter or margarine

10 eggs

⅛ teaspoon white pepper

4 ounces smoked salmon, flaked

6 tablespoons half-and-half or milk

4 dashes Worcestershire sauce

4 drops Tabasco sauce

Melt butter or margarine in a double boiler. In a bowl, whisk eggs. Add pepper, salmon, half-and-half, Worcestershire sauce, and Tabasco sauce. Pour egg mixture into the double boiler and stir until thick and creamy. Serve immediately.

FOUR SERVINGS

HAWAIIAN SCRAMBLE

THE OLD BRICK SILO BED & BREAKFAST

LEAVENWORTH, WASHINGTON

10 eggs

Salt and pepper to taste

1½ cups cooked ham, cubed (½- to ¾-inch cubes)

¾ cup pineapple tidbits, drained

1½ cups shredded Swiss cheese

Preheat broiler. In a large bowl, beat eggs with salt and pepper. Pour into a lightly greased nonstick skillet. Stir eggs over medium heat until set but still soft. Warm ham cubes in a separate skillet and add to eggs along with pineapple and 1 cup of the cheese; continue to cook until eggs are set. Spoon eggs into 4 au gratin dishes. Sprinkle with remaining cheese and broil just until cheese is melted. Serve immediately.

FOUR SERVINGS

CHEESE, APPLE, AND AMARETTO OMELET

BLACKBERRY INN

SEAL ROCK, OREGON

4 eggs, at room temperature

2 tablespoons cream or milk

Dash of salt and pepper (optional)

2 teaspoons butter

FILLING:

2 tablespoons butter

3 tablespoons sugar

1 Golden Delicious apple, peeled, cored, and thinly sliced

1 tablespoon amaretto liqueur or ½ teaspoon almond extract

1½ ounces cream cheese, softened

For filling, melt butter in a medium skillet. Stir in sugar and apple and sauté until apples are tender. Stir in liqueur or extract and remove from heat. Cover and set aside to keep warm. Beat together eggs, cream, and salt and pepper, if desired. Melt 1 teaspoon of the butter in a hot omelet pan. Pour half of the egg mixture into pan. When eggs have set, cover with half of apple mixture. Top with half of cream cheese, and continue cooking for 1 minute. Fold or roll omelet and slide out of pan onto a heated serving dish. Repeat with remaining ingredients to make second omelet. Serve immediately.

TWO SERVINGS

APPLE AND SAUSAGE OMELET

CHANNEL HOUSE BED & BREAKFAST

ANACORTES, WASHINGTON

5 teaspoons unsalted butter

4 breakfast sausage links, cut into ¼-inch slices

1 Idaho potato, peeled and thinly sliced

1 onion, sliced and separated into rings

1 Granny Smith apple, peeled, cored, and thinly sliced

6 eggs

¼ cup water

2 tablespoons chopped parsley

1 tablespoon olive oil

1 teaspoon freshly ground pepper

In a small heavy skillet, melt 1 teaspoon of the butter over medium heat. Add sausage slices and sauté until browned. Drain on a paper towel; set aside. Melt remaining 4 teaspoons butter in a 10-inch nonstick skillet. Add potato and onion and cook over low heat for 5 minutes. Add apple and cook another 5 minutes, stirring occasionally. In a separate bowl, whisk eggs together with water and 1 tablespoon of the parsley. Add oil, pepper, and reserved sausage to skillet. Pour in egg mixture and swirl pan to spread eggs evenly. Cover skillet and cook over medium heat for 15 minutes, or until eggs are just set. Carefully invert omelet onto serving platter. Sprinkle with remaining 1 tablespoon parsley. Serve immediately.

FOUR SERVINGS

BAKED EGGS FLORENTINE

BLUE HOUSE INN

LANGLEY, WASHINGTON

16 to 20 fresh spinach leaves

1 teaspoon butter

4 tablespoons grated Parmesan cheese

4 large eggs

4 tablespoons whipping cream

Freshly ground pepper

Preheat oven to 375 degrees. Spray 4 ramekins with nonstick cooking spray. Lightly steam spinach leaves in butter until wilted; let cool. Line ramekins with spinach leaves. Place 1 teaspoon of the Parmesan over each bed of spinach. Gently crack an egg into each ramekin. Pour 1 tablespoon of cream around the edge of each egg. Sprinkle with remaining 2 tablespoons plus 2 teaspoons cheese and a dash of pepper. Bake for 10 to 12 minutes, until eggs are firm.

FOUR SERVINGS

FEATHER BED GOLDENROD EGGS

THE FEATHER BED

QUINCY, CALIFORNIA

5 hard-boiled eggs

1 tablespoon butter

2 tablespoons all-purpose flour

1 cup milk

Pinch each salt and pepper

½ cup sour cream

1 tablespoon Dijon mustard

1 cup sliced mushrooms, sautéed

1 cup shredded cheese (Cheddar, Monterey jack, or Swiss)

3 English muffins, split

6 slices tomato

6 slices Canadian bacon

Shell hard-boiled eggs. Dice whites; set aside. Mash yolks until crumbly; set aside. In a medium saucepan, melt butter. Gradually stir in flour to make a paste. Add milk and seasonings; stir until smooth. Continue cooking, stirring frequently, until sauce thickens. Add sour cream, mustard, and cheese, stirring until blended. Add sautéed mushrooms and diced egg whites; remove from heat; cover. Toast and butter English muffins. To assemble, place a tomato slice on 6 of the English muffin halves. Follow with a slice of Canadian bacon. Top with sauce, and sprinkle with crumbled egg yolk.

SIX SERVINGS

BAKED HERB-CHEESE EGGS

THE FLEMING JONES HOMESTEAD

PLACERVILLE, CALIFORNIA

1 tablespoon butter, melted

1 egg

1 to 2 tablespoons half-and-half

1 tablespoon shredded sharp Cheddar, jack, or Swiss cheese

1 teaspoon grated Parmesan cheese

Pinch each oregano, basil, parsley, pepper, and paprika

Preheat oven to 350 degrees. Pour melted butter into ramekin or custard cup. Break egg into dish. Pour half-and-half around edges of yolk. Sprinkle cheese and herbs on top of cream. Place ramekin in a large pan filled with 1 inch of hot water. Place in oven and bake for 15 to 20 minutes, until cream and cheese begin to bubble. Serve immediately.

ONE SERVING

SEASHELL
EGG
BAKE

LOG CASTLE BED & BREAKFAST

LANGLEY, WASHINGTON

½ slice bacon, fried

½ cup shredded Swiss cheese

1 egg

1 teaspoon whipping cream

Salt and pepper to taste

Preheat oven to 350 degrees. Crumble bacon into small pieces; set aside. Spray a 3-inch-long seashell with nonstick cooking spray. Sprinkle three-fourths of the cheese on bottom of shell. Crack egg onto bed of cheese. Add cream, salt, and pepper to top of egg. Sprinkle with fried bacon bits and remaining cheese. Bake for 10 minutes, until egg is firm. Serve immediately.

ONE SERVING

BAKED EGG SURPRISE

MARJON BED & BREAKFAST INN

LEABURG, OREGON

1½ tablespoons whipping cream

1 extra-large egg

Dash each salt and pepper

2 tablespoons shredded Havarti cheese

8 caraway seeds

3 small frozen sausage links

1 tablespoon baby green peas, fresh or frozen (thawed if frozen)

Preheat oven to 425 degrees. Spray a ramekin or custard cup with non-stick cooking spray. Pour cream into bottom of cup. Crack egg into cup, being careful not to break yolk. Sprinkle egg with salt, pepper, and cheese. Sprinkle caraway seeds on top of cheese. Bake for 8 to 10 minutes, or until white of egg is firm but yolk still jiggles. Meanwhile, cut sausage links into ¼-inch slices and fry until well cooked; drain well. Remove egg from oven and top with peas and sausage pieces. Serve immediately.

ONE SERVING

HAM AND EGGS WITH SHERRY

NORTH COAST COUNTRY INN

GUALALA, CALIFORNIA

3 thick slices ham, diced

16 eggs

½ cup half-and-half

¼ cup dry sherry

1 teaspoon Worcestershire sauce

⅛ teaspoon cayenne pepper

2 cups shredded Monterey jack cheese

Paprika

Preheat oven to 350 degrees. Grease 8 ramekins or custard cups. Cover bottoms of dishes with ham. Break 2 eggs over top of ham in each dish. In a small bowl, stir together half-and-half, sherry, Worcestershire sauce, and cayenne; pour equally over eggs. Place ramekins on a cookie sheet and bake for 10 minutes, or just until eggs are set. Sprinkle with cheese and a dash of paprika. Continue baking for 10 to 15 minutes, until eggs are firm. Serve immediately.

EIGHT SERVINGS

BAKED EGGS ON TOAST

ST. HELENS MANORHOUSE

MORTON, WASHINGTON

6 slices whole-grain bread

6 large eggs

2 to 3 tablespoons butter

Salt and pepper to taste

Shredded Cheddar cheese and chopped green onions (optional)

WHITE SAUCE:

4 tablespoons all-purpose flour

1 cup milk

2 tablespoons butter

Salt to taste

Preheat oven to 350 degrees. For sauce, combine flour with enough water to make a thin paste; stir until smooth. In a small saucepan, scald milk. Add flour mixture, butter, and salt to scalded milk and cook over low heat, stirring constantly, until thickened. Set aside. Toast bread slices, and cut each slice into a large circle. Lightly butter both sides. Cut a small hole (approximately 1½ inches in diameter) from the center of each bread circle. Place bread on a greased rimmed cookie sheet. Break an egg into the hole in each piece of bread. Place a dot of butter on top of each egg, and sprinkle with salt and pepper. Spoon sauce over eggs, reserving ½ cup. Bake for 10 minutes, until eggs are firm. To serve, carefully place eggs on a platter or plate and surround with reserved sauce. Sprinkle with cheese and green onions, if desired.

SIX SERVINGS

MINIATURE HAM AND CHEESE QUICHES

THE PRINGLE HOUSE

BED & BREAKFAST

OAKLAND, OREGON

CRUST:

½ cup butter or margarine, softened

3 ounces cream cheese, softened

1 cup all-purpose flour

FILLING:

2¼ -ounce can deviled ham

1 small onion, chopped

1 teaspoon butter or margarine

¼ cup shredded Swiss cheese

1 egg, slightly beaten

¼ cup milk

½ teaspoon nutmeg

Dash pepper

Preheat oven to 450 degrees. For crust, in a bowl, combine butter or margarine and cream cheese; beat until fluffy. Gradually add the flour, mixing until smooth. Chill thoroughly. Divide and shape dough into twelve 1-inch balls. Press dough evenly into 12 miniature muffin cups (1⅞ inches diameter). For filling, spoon a little deviled ham into each cup. In a skillet, lightly sauté onion in butter or margarine. Mix onion with half of the cheese and sprinkle over ham. In a small bowl, combine the remaining cheese, egg, milk, nutmeg, and pepper. Spoon egg mixture evenly into the cups. Bake for 10 minutes, then reduce heat to 350 degrees and bake for 15 minutes, or until custard is set. Serve warm.

Note: Cooled quiches can easily be frozen. To reheat, bake at 350 degrees for 15 minutes.

TWELVE MINIATURE QUICHES

CASSEROLES, QUICHES, AND FRITTATAS

BAKED CHILES RELLENOS

ROMEO INN

ASHLAND, OREGON

1½ pounds lean ground beef

1 cup chopped onion

Salt and pepper to taste

12 ounces canned diced green chiles

4½ cups shredded Cheddar cheese

3¾ cups milk

10 eggs, beaten

1¼ cups all-purpose flour

1 teaspoon salt

Dash pepper

Several dashes Tabasco sauce

Preheat oven to 350 degrees. In a skillet, brown the ground beef and onion; drain well. Season the meat mixture to taste with salt and pepper. Place half of the chiles in a greased 10- by 13-inch baking dish. Cover the chiles with the cheese and the meat mixture. Top with remaining chiles. In a bowl, combine milk, eggs, flour, salt, pepper, and Tabasco sauce, and beat until smooth. Pour over chiles. Bake for 45 to 50 minutes, until eggs are set.

TWELVE SERVINGS

BAKED CHEESE OMELET

WHISPERING PINES

SPOKANE, WASHINGTON

12 eggs

1 cup milk

Dash salt

Drop of Tabasco

2 cups shredded Cheddar cheese

2 cups shredded Monterey jack cheese or mozzarella cheese

Preheat oven to 325 degrees. In a blender or bowl, beat eggs, milk, salt, Tabasco, and cheese. Pour egg mixture into an ungreased 8-inch round soufflé dish. Bake for approximately 1 hour, until eggs are set.

EIGHT SERVINGS

PEPPERONI EGG CASSEROLE

HEALDSBURG INN ON THE PLAZA

HEALDSBURG, CALIFORNIA

2 cups unseasoned bread cubes

1 cup shredded Monterey jack cheese

5 eggs

2 cups milk

1 teaspoon Italian seasoning

⅓ cup chopped pepperoni

Preheat oven to 325 degrees. Place bread cubes in the bottom of a greased 6- by 10-inch baking dish. Cover with cheese. In a large bowl, combine eggs, milk, and seasoning; pour over bread and cheese. Top with pepperoni. Bake for 35 to 45 minutes, until set.

SIX SERVINGS

CHILE CHEESE BAKE

MARGIE'S BED & BREAKFAST

SEQUIM, WASHINGTON

6 slices of bread, buttered and crusts trimmed

2 cups shredded sharp Cheddar cheese

2 cups shredded Monterey jack cheese

4 ounces canned diced green chiles

6 eggs

2 cups milk

2 teaspoons paprika

1 teaspoon salt

½ teaspoon pepper

½ teaspoon oregano

¼ teaspoon garlic powder

¼ teaspoon dry mustard

Preheat oven to 325 degrees. Place bread, buttered side down, in a greased 9- by 13-inch baking dish. Combine cheeses and scatter on top of bread. Sprinkle chiles on top of cheese. In a medium bowl, beat eggs with milk and seasonings; pour over cheese and let soak into bread. Cover and refrigerate at least 4 hours. Bake for 55 minutes, until golden brown.

TEN SERVINGS

MORNING CASSEROLE

PENSIONE NICHOLS

SEATTLE, WASHINGTON

16 slices white bread, crusts trimmed

16 slices Canadian bacon or ham

16 slices sharp Cheddar cheese

6 eggs

½ teaspoon each salt, pepper, and dry mustard

¼ cup minced onion

¼ cup finely chopped green pepper

1 to 2 teaspoons Worcestershire sauce

3 cups whole milk

Dash Tabasco sauce

TOPPING:

½ cup butter

¾ cup crushed cornflakes

In a greased 9- by 13-inch glass baking dish, place 8 slices of bread in one layer. Top bread with slices of bacon or ham and follow with a layer of cheese. Place remaining bread slices over cheese. In a bowl, beat eggs with salt, pepper, and dry mustard. Add onion, green pepper, Worcestershire sauce, milk, and Tabasco sauce; pour over bread mixture. Cover and refrigerate overnight.

Next day, preheat oven to 350 degrees. For topping, melt butter and pour over casserole. Top with a layer of crushed cornflakes. Bake, uncovered, for 1 hour, until golden brown. Remove from oven and let stand 10 minutes before serving.

EIGHT SERVINGS

SAUSAGE STRATA

PORTAGE INLET HOUSE

BED & BREAKFAST

VICTORIA, BRITISH COLUMBIA

1 pound sausage meat

2 to 3 green onions, finely chopped

2 slices bread, cubed

1 cup shredded Cheddar cheese

6 eggs

1½ cups milk

In a skillet, cook sausage and onion; drain well. Place cubed bread in a greased 9-inch-square baking dish. Sprinkle sausage mixture over bread, then top with ¾ cup of the shredded cheese. In a bowl, combine eggs and milk; pour over bread mixture. Top with remaining ¼ cup cheese. Refrigerate overnight. Next day, preheat oven to 350 degrees and bake for 1 hour, until set.

SIX SERVINGS

CORN CASSEROLE

NORTH GARDEN INN

BELLINGHAM, WASHINGTON

4 cups (16 oz.) fresh or frozen corn

3 eggs, lightly beaten

½ cup all-purpose flour

1 cup milk

4 ounces canned diced green chiles

½ teaspoon garlic powder

Salt and pepper to taste

1 cup shredded Cheddar cheese

Preheat oven to 350 degrees. In a large bowl, combine corn, eggs, flour, milk, chiles, garlic powder, and salt and pepper. Pour into a greased 9-inch-square casserole dish. Top with cheese. Bake for 45 minutes, until top is golden.

TEN SERVINGS

CRUSTLESS MUSHROOM QUICHE

AMBER HOUSE

SACRAMENTO, CALIFORNIA

½ pound mushrooms, sliced

1 bunch green onions, chopped

3 tablespoons butter or margarine

3 eggs

½ cup plus 1 tablespoon biscuit mix

½ teaspoon salt

¼ teaspoon pepper

½ teaspoon nutmeg

1½ cups milk

1½ cups shredded Monterey jack cheese

Preheat oven to 350 degrees. Sauté mushrooms and onions in butter or margarine. In a large bowl, beat eggs. Add biscuit mix, salt, pepper, and nutmeg; beat 1 minute. Slowly add milk to egg mixture and blend thoroughly. Place half of the mushrooms and onions in the bottom of a greased 9-inch quiche dish. Top with cheese, followed by remaining mushrooms and onions. Pour egg mixture over top. Bake for 30 to 35 minutes, until set.

SIX SERVINGS

APPLE-RAISIN QUICHE

ARBOR HOUSE BY THE SEA

MANZANITA, OREGON

10-inch unbaked pie shell

¼ cup raisins

3 large apples, peeled, cored, and thinly sliced

2 eggs

1 cup whipping cream

⅛ cup sugar

1 teaspoon cinnamon

Preheat oven to 475 degrees. Bake pie shell until light brown. Sprinkle bottom of pie shell with raisins. Top with apples. In a large bowl, mix eggs, cream, sugar, and cinnamon; pour over apples. Bake for 10 minutes, then reduce heat to 350 degrees and bake for 50 minutes longer, until set.

SIX SERVINGS

GARDEN MEDLEY QUICHE

BEAZLEY HOUSE

NAPA, CALIFORNIA

10 eggs

½ cup all-purpose flour

1 teaspoon baking powder

1½ teaspoons onion powder

½ teaspoon garlic powder

¼ cup butter or margarine, melted

3 cups cottage cheese

1 cup cooked fresh spinach or 10 ounces frozen chopped spinach, thawed and squeezed dry

½ red pepper, chopped

½ yellow or green pepper, chopped

1 bunch green onions, chopped

12 ounces shredded Swiss or Monterey jack cheese

Preheat oven to 350 degrees. In a blender or food processor, combine eggs, flour, baking powder, onion powder, garlic powder, butter or margarine, and 1 cup of the cottage cheese; blend well. Pour blended mixture into a large bowl and add remaining cottage cheese, spinach, peppers, green onions, and shredded cheese. Mix all ingredients thoroughly. Divide mixture between 2 greased 10-inch pie pans. Bake for 40 to 45 minutes, until set.

TWELVE SERVINGS

SOUTH OF THE BORDER QUICHE

SALISBURY HOUSE

SEATTLE, WASHINGTON

6 eggs

2 tablespoons all-purpose flour

2 cups cottage cheese

1 cup shredded Monterey jack cheese

¼ cup butter or margarine, melted

4 ounces canned diced green chiles

Salsa and sour cream (optional)

Preheat oven to 375 degrees. In a large bowl, beat eggs. Add flour. Mix in cottage cheese, jack cheese, butter, and chiles. Pour into a greased 10-inch pie pan. Bake for 30 minutes, until set. Serve with salsa and sour cream, if desired.

SIX SERVINGS

FANTASTIC SPINACH DELIGHT

FRANKLIN HOUSE BED & BREAKFAST INN

ASTORIA, OREGON

1½ cups biscuit mix

½ cup milk

5 eggs

1 small onion, chopped

½ cup grated Parmesan cheese

1¼ cups shredded Cheddar cheese

2 cups cottage cheese

2 teaspoons minced garlic

1 cup cooked spinach, drained well and patted dry

¾ cup shredded Cheddar cheese, for topping

In a large bowl, combine biscuit mix, milk, and 2 of the eggs. Add onion. Spread mixture in the bottom of a greased 9- by 13-inch baking dish. In a bowl, mix together Parmesan and Cheddar cheese, cottage cheese, garlic, spinach, and remaining 3 eggs. Carefully spoon over first layer. Cover and refrigerate overnight. Next day, preheat oven to 350 degrees. Bake for 30 minutes, until set. Remove from oven. Let stand for several minutes before cutting. Sprinkle each serving with 1 tablespoon Cheddar cheese.

TWELVE SERVINGS

SMOKED SALMON CHEESECAKE

WHITE SWAN INN

SAN FRANCISCO, CALIFORNIA

CRUST:

1½ tablespoons butter

½ cup bread crumbs, toasted

¼ cup shredded Gruyère cheese

1 teaspoon chopped fresh dill, or ¼ teaspoon dried

FILLING:

1 onion, finely chopped

3 tablespoons butter

28 ounces cream cheese, at room temperature

4 eggs

⅓ cup half-and-half

½ cup shredded Gruyère cheese

8 ounces smoked salmon, flaked

Salt to taste

Preheat oven to 325 degrees. For crust, spread butter on bottom and sides of a 9-inch springform pan. In a bowl, mix bread crumbs, cheese, and dill together, and sprinkle mixture in pan, turning to coat. Refrigerate. For filling, in a skillet, sauté onion in butter. Using a mixer, in a large bowl, beat cream cheese and eggs until fluffy. Beat in half-and-half. Fold in cheese, onion, and salmon. Add salt to taste. Pour into prepared pan. Set the pan in a large roasting pan and add hot water halfway up the sides of the springform pan. Bake for 1 hour and 20 minutes, until set. Turn oven off and let cheesecake cool in oven with door ajar for 1 hour. Transfer pan to cooling rack. Let cool to room temperature before serving.

FOURTEEN SERVINGS

SPINACH FRITTATA

CALISTOGA'S WINE WAY INN

CALISTOGA, CALIFORNIA

½ cup butter

6 eggs

1 cup buttermilk baking mix

1 cup milk

4 cups shredded Monterey jack cheese

20 ounces frozen chopped spinach, thawed and squeezed dry or 2 cups cooked fresh spinach

Preheat oven to 350 degrees. Melt butter in a 7- by 11-inch baking dish. In a bowl, beat eggs with baking mix and milk. Stir in cheese and spinach, blending well. Pour mixture into baking dish. Bake for 40 minutes, until golden brown. Cool for 5 to 10 minutes before serving. Note: This frittata freezes well.

TEN SERVINGS

ARTICHOKE-BACON FRITTATA

STEIGER HAUS

McMINNVILLE, OREGON

1 small onion, chopped

2 tablespoons butter

Two 6½-ounce jars marinated artichoke hearts, drained and chopped (reserve liquid from one jar)

6 eggs

⅓ cup grated Parmesan cheese

⅓ cup bread crumbs

6 slices bacon, cooked and crumbled

½ cup shredded Monterey jack cheese (optional)

Preheat oven to 325 degrees. In a skillet, sauté onion in butter until transparent; add artichokes and the liquid from one jar. Heat for 2 minutes. In a bowl, lightly beat eggs; add cheese, bread crumbs, artichoke mixture, and bacon. Mix together and place in a greased 9-inch quiche pan. Bake for 25 minutes, until set. Sprinkle frittata with jack cheese, if desired, and bake for 5 more minutes.

SIX SERVINGS

FRENCH TOAST, PANCAKES, AND WAFFLES

ORANGE MARNIER FRENCH TOAST

BRANNAN COTTAGE INN

CALISTOGA, CALIFORNIA

4 eggs plus 2 egg whites

½ cup sugar

¼ teaspoon salt

3 cups milk

1 tablespoon Grand Marnier liqueur

Grated rind of 1 orange

1 loaf sweet French bread, cut into twelve 1-inch-thick slices

Sprinkle of nutmeg

Confectioners' sugar

In a large bowl, whisk together eggs, egg whites, sugar, and salt. Stir in milk, Grand Marnier, and orange rind. Soak bread in egg mixture until thoroughly saturated, about 1 minute. Arrange slices on a baking sheet and sprinkle lightly with nutmeg; let stand 1 hour. Preheat oven to 400 degrees. In a large, lightly greased skillet or on a heated, oiled griddle, slowly brown both sides of bread, 2 to 3 minutes on each side. Place on a clean baking sheet and bake for 20 minutes. Sprinkle generously with confectioners' sugar. Serve with butter and syrup.

SIX SERVINGS

SURPRISE FRENCH TOAST

CEDARYM BED & BREAKFAST

REDMOND, WASHINGTON

1 loaf day-old French bread, cut into twelve 1-inch-thick slices

¾ cup orange marmalade

*4 eggs, lightly beaten**

2 tablespoons milk

2 tablespoons triple sec liqueur

1 tablespoon maple syrup

1½ teaspoons grated orange rind

½ teaspoon nutmeg

Safflower oil, for frying

Confectioners' sugar

Make a pocket slit in each slice of bread. Fill each pocket with 1 tablespoon orange marmalade. In a bowl, combine eggs, milk, liqueur, maple syrup, grated orange rind, and nutmeg; pour into a shallow dish. Dip each bread slice into egg mixture and let soak thoroughly. Heat griddle. Fry bread in a shallow layer of safflower oil for 2 to 5 minutes on each side, until golden brown. Transfer to serving platter and sprinkle with confectioners' sugar.

*Use an equivalent amount of egg substitute in place of the eggs, if desired.

SIX SERVINGS

FRESH PEACH FRENCH TOAST

THE MORICAL HOUSE

ASHLAND, OREGON

4 eggs

1 cup half-and-half

¼ cup sugar

8 slices French bread, ½ inch thick

Butter for frying

6 fresh peaches, peeled and sliced

½ cup fresh raspberries

¼ cup sliced almonds, toasted

Confectioners' sugar or whipped cream (optional)

In a medium bowl, whisk together eggs, half-and-half, and sugar. Place bread slices in a shallow pan and pour egg mixture over top. Turn bread over to saturate thoroughly. Cover and refrigerate overnight. Next day, melt 4 tablespoons butter on a hot griddle. Fry bread 4 to 5 minutes on each side, until golden brown. To serve, top with peaches, raspberries, and sliced almonds. Sprinkle with confectioners' sugar or top with a dollop of whipped cream, if desired.

FOUR SERVINGS

DECADENT FRENCH TOAST

WILLOWS INN

LUMMI ISLAND, WASHINGTON

2 (day-old) croissants

¼ cup cream cheese

8 fresh strawberries

3 eggs

½ cup half-and-half

3 tablespoons sugar

1 teaspoon vanilla extract

Butter or margarine, for frying

Confectioners' sugar

Slice croissants lengthwise to make a butterfly shape. Spread 1 tablespoon cream cheese on the inside of each croissant half. Slice 4 strawberries and place slices on cream cheese. Fold halves together to re-form croissants. In a medium bowl, whisk together eggs, half-and-half, sugar, and vanilla extract. Soak croissants, dipping both sides in batter, but do not allow them to become soggy. In a skillet, fry croissants on both sides in butter or margarine until thoroughly cooked and golden brown. Garnish with remaining berries sliced into fan shapes (leave green hull intact). Dust liberally with confectioners' sugar.

TWO SERVINGS

ALMOND PANCAKES

BENNETT HOUSE BED & BREAKFAST

PORT ANGELES, WASHINGTON

4 cups buttermilk pancake mix (such as Krusteaz)

3 cups water

1 teaspoon almond extract

½ cup sliced almonds

In a bowl, stir together pancake mix, water, and almond extract. Add more water if a thinner pancake is desired. Beat until smooth. (There will be some small lumps.) Add almonds. Heat griddle, and oil if necessary. Pour ⅓ cup batter onto griddle. Flip when bubbles appear on surface. Brown on both sides. Serve with maple syrup heated with a few drops of almond extract.

EIGHTEEN PANCAKES

GINGER PANCAKES WITH LEMON SAUCE

CHELSEA STATION BED & BREAKFAST INN

SEATTLE, WASHINGTON

PANCAKES:

4 cups whole wheat and honey pancake mix (such as Krusteaz)

2 teaspoons ground ginger

1 teaspoon cinnamon

½ teaspoon nutmeg

¼ teaspoon ground cloves

2 teaspoons molasses

3½ cups water

LEMON SAUCE:

1 cup sugar

2 tablespoons cornstarch

2 cups water

¼ cup butter

2 tablespoons grated lemon rind

¼ cup lemon juice

For sauce, combine sugar and cornstarch in a medium saucepan. Gradually stir in water. Bring to a boil. Cook over medium heat, stirring constantly, for 5 minutes, or until thickened. Remove from heat. Add butter, lemon rind, and lemon juice; mix well. Keep warm. For pancakes, in a large bowl, whisk together pancake mix, spices, molasses, and water; blend until smooth. Heat griddle, and oil if necessary. Pour batter onto hot griddle, forming medium-sized pancakes. When bubbles form on surface, flip and brown other side. Serve with warm Lemon Sauce.

EIGHTEEN PANCAKES

HUCKLEBERRY PANCAKES

FLYING L RANCH

GLENWOOD, WASHINGTON

8 cups unbleached all-purpose flour

2 cups old-fashioned rolled oats

2 cups All-Bran cereal

¼ cup baking powder

2 tablespoons baking soda

2 tablespoons salt

1 dozen eggs

¾ cup vegetable oil

3 quarts buttermilk

6 cups huckleberries or other fruit

In a large bowl, combine flour, oats, cereal, baking powder, baking soda, and salt. (Mixture can be stored in an air-tight container for future use.) For every 1 cup dry mix, add 1 egg, 1 tablespoon oil, and 1 cup buttermilk; mix well. Fold in ½ cup huckleberries. Heat griddle, and oil if necessary. Pour ¼ cup batter onto hot griddle and cook until bubbly. Flip and cook other side until golden brown. Serve with butter and syrup, or fruit spread.

4 DOZEN PANCAKES

BANANA BUCKWHEAT BUTTERMILK PANCAKES

TEN INVERNESS WAY

INVERNESS, CALIFORNIA

1 cup all-purpose flour

1 cup whole wheat flour

1 cup buckwheat flour

3 tablespoons sugar

2 tablespoons baking powder

1½ teaspoons baking soda

¾ teaspoon salt

3 eggs

6 tablespoons vegetable oil

3 cups buttermilk

3 ripe bananas, mashed

In a large bowl, combine flours, sugar, baking powder, baking soda, and salt. In a separate bowl, beat eggs, oil, and buttermilk; add bananas. Add wet ingredients to dry ingredients and stir to combine. Heat griddle, and oil if necessary. Pour ¼ cup batter onto hot griddle. When bubbles form on surface, flip and brown on other side. Serve with butter and maple syrup.

THIRTY-SIX PANCAKES

APPLE-WALNUT WHOLE WHEAT PANCAKES

MOUNT ASHLAND INN

ASHLAND, OREGON

⅔ cup milk

2 tablespoons butter or margarine, melted

2 tablespoons molasses

1 egg

⅔ cup all-purpose flour

⅓ cup whole wheat flour

2 teaspoons baking powder

¼ teaspoon salt

¼ cup chopped walnuts

½ green apple, peeled, cored, and diced

In a large bowl, lightly beat together milk, butter, molasses, and egg. In a separate bowl, sift together flours, baking powder, and salt. Add nuts and apple to dry ingredients. Add dry ingredients to wet ingredients and mix just until blended. If necessary, add milk to make batter the consistency of whipping cream. Heat griddle, and oil if necessary. Pour ¼ cup batter onto hot griddle. Flip when bubbles form on surface. Cook on other side until golden brown. Serve with butter and maple syrup.

TEN TO TWELVE PANCAKES

BLUE CORN PANCAKES WITH PINEAPPLE SALSA

RANCHO CAYMUS INN

RUTHERFORD, CALIFORNIA

PANCAKES:

1 cup blue cornmeal

2 tablespoons sugar

½ teaspoon salt

1 cup boiling water

1 egg

¾ cup milk

2 tablespoons butter, melted

½ cup all-purpose flour

2 teaspoons baking powder

PINEAPPLE SALSA:

1 fresh whole pineapple

1 cup corn syrup

½ cup dried currants

½ cup dried cherries

Juice and grated rind of 1 lime

For salsa, cut pineapple into small chunks. Place in a bowl along with any juice extracted from cutting. Add corn syrup, dried fruit, lime juice, and grated rind; mix well. Set aside.

For pancakes, in a large bowl, stir together cornmeal, sugar, salt, and boiling water. Let sit 10 minutes. In a separate bowl, beat together egg, milk, and butter; add to cornmeal mixture. Sift flour and baking powder; add to batter and mix well. Heat griddle, and oil if necessary. Pour ¼ cup batter onto hot griddle and cook until bubbly. Flip and cook other side until golden brown. Serve with salsa or maple syrup.

TWELVE PANCAKES

SWEDISH PANCAKES WITH HUCKLEBERRY SAUCE

WAVERLY PLACE BED & BREAKFAST

SPOKANE, WASHINGTON

PANCAKES:

2 eggs, beaten

1 cup milk

1 cup all-purpose flour

1 teaspoon sugar

¼ teaspoon salt

⅓ cup butter

HUCKLEBERRY SAUCE:

½ cup sugar

1½ tablespoons cornstarch

2 cups huckleberries

⅓ cup water

2 tablespoons lemon juice

For sauce, combine sugar and cornstarch in a medium saucepan; stir in berries. Add water and lemon juice and cook over medium heat until thickened. For pancakes, in a medium bowl, combine eggs, milk, flour, sugar, and salt; beat until smooth. Melt butter in an 8- or 9-inch cast-iron skillet; add to batter. Heat skillet over medium-high heat, and pour ¼ cup batter into pan. Turn to coat bottom of pan. Flip to brown on both sides. Roll up pancake and keep warm in oven. Repeat with remaining batter. Serve with Huckleberry Sauce, jam, or syrup.

EIGHT PANCAKES

APPLE-FILLED CRÊPES

FOOTHILL HOUSE

CALISTOGA, CALIFORNIA

CRÊPES:

1½ cups milk

3 eggs

1¼ cups all-purpose flour

¼ teaspoon cinnamon

2 tablespoons butter, melted

APPLE FILLING:

4 apples, peeled, cored, and sliced

2 tablespoons packed brown sugar

2 tablespoons butter or margarine

½ cup raisins

1 teaspoon cinnamon

2 tablespoons amaretto liqueur

For crêpes, combine milk, eggs, flour, and cinnamon in blender or food processor. With motor running, add melted butter. Let sit at room temperature for 1 hour. Pour ¼ cup batter into an 8-inch nonstick skillet and cook over medium-low heat, allowing batter to spread over entire bottom of pan. Turn and brown crêpe on other side. Transfer to a plate. Repeat procedure with remaining batter. Note: Crêpes can be stored in refrigerator for up to 1 week. For filling, in a skillet, sauté apples with sugar in butter or margarine for 5 minutes. Add raisins, cinnamon, and amaretto; mix well. Remove from heat. Spoon ¼ to ⅓ cup apple filling onto each warm crêpe, and roll crêpe loosely. Sprinkle with cinnamon.

TWELVE CRÊPES

APPLE FRITTERS

CARTER HOUSE

EUREKA, CALIFORNIA

2 cups all-purpose flour

1 tablespoon sugar

½ teaspoon salt

12-ounce bottle of beer

2 egg whites

2 large apples, peeled, cored, and sliced

Oil, for frying

Whipped cream or maple syrup (optional)

In a large bowl, mix flour, sugar, and salt. Add beer and mix until smooth. In a separate bowl, beat egg whites until stiff; fold into beer mixture. Let batter rest in refrigerator for at least 30 minutes. In a deep skillet, heat at least 1 inch of oil to at least 375 degrees. Dip apple slices in batter, coating completely. Place in oil and cook for 2 minutes, or until golden brown. Remove and place on paper towel. Serve fritters warm with whipped cream or maple syrup, if desired.

FOUR SERVINGS

FRANK'S WHOLE WHEAT WAFFLES

STATE STREET INN

HOOD RIVER, OREGON

2 cups whole wheat flour

2 teaspoons baking powder

3 eggs, separated

1½ cups whole milk

½ cup butter, melted

Fresh strawberries and whipped cream (optional)

Preheat waffle iron. In a large bowl, mix flour and baking powder; set aside. In a medium bowl, combine egg yolks, milk, and butter. In a separate bowl, beat egg whites until stiff. Add milk mixture to flour; mix just until blended. Fold in egg whites. Cook in hot waffle iron until golden brown. Serve with strawberries and whipped cream, if desired.

FOUR 7-INCH WAFFLES

BUCKWHEAT BUTTERMILK WAFFLES

TURTLEBACK FARM INN

ORCAS ISLAND, WASHINGTON

¾ cup buckwheat flour

½ cup unbleached white flour

¼ cup whole wheat flour

2 teaspoons baking powder

¾ teaspoon baking soda

½ teaspoon salt

2 tablespoons sugar

3 eggs

1½ cups buttermilk

½ cup butter, melted and cooled

Preheat waffle iron. In a large bowl, combine flours, baking powder, baking soda, salt, and sugar. In a separate bowl, beat eggs, buttermilk, and butter. Add buttermilk mixture to dry ingredients; mix just until blended. Cook in hot waffle iron until golden brown. Serve with butter and pure maple syrup.

FOUR 7-INCH WAFFLES

FRUITS, SAUCES, AND SMOOTHIES

PEARS EXTRAORDINAIRE

HOME BY THE SEA

CLINTON, WASHINGTON

⅓ cup cream cheese, softened

1 tablespoon honey

1 teaspoon vanilla extract

2 firm fresh pears, peeled

2 tablespoons water

In a small bowl, combine cream cheese, honey, and vanilla extract; set aside. Peel and cut pears in half lengthwise, and remove core. Place cut side down in a microwave-safe baking dish. Add the water. Poach in microwave at full power until pears are soft, 2 to 3 minutes. Spoon one-fourth of cream cheese mixture into each pear half. Serve immediately.

FOUR SERVINGS

BROWN SUGAR SUNSHINE

F. W. HASTINGS HOUSE

OLD CONSULATE INN

PORT TOWNSEND, WASHINGTON

1 medium grapefruit

2 generous tablespoons port wine

2 tablespoons light brown sugar

2 tablespoons butter, melted

Preheat broiler. Cut grapefruit in half. Run a knife along the inner contours of the rind to remove the flesh in one piece. Reserve rind, and place skinned grapefruit mound upside down on cutting surface; cut like a pie into 6 sections. Replace grapefruit in shell and place in baking dish. Spoon 1 tablespoon port on each half. Cover surface with 1 tablespoon sugar per half. Drizzle with butter. Let stand a few minutes (the longer the better). Broil 10 minutes, until bubbly and golden brown. Place each half in a small bowl and top with remaining liquid from baking dish.

TWO SERVINGS

WASHINGTON BAKED PEARS

ORCHARD HILL INN

WHITE SALMON, WASHINGTON

6 medium-sized fresh pears

¼ cup packed brown sugar

¼ teaspoon cinnamon

¼ teaspoon nutmeg

½ cup whole pecans

½ cup raisins

2 tablespoons butter

Sour cream, plain yogurt, or whipped cream (optional)

Preheat oven to 375 degrees. Core each pear, leaving bottom intact. Cut a hairline circle around the middle of each pear, just piercing the skin. In a small bowl, combine sugar, spices, nuts, and raisins. Fill pears with mixture and dot with butter. Arrange pears upright in a small baking dish. Pour ½ inch water into bottom of dish. Bake for 45 to 55 minutes, until pears are tender. Cool for 15 minutes. Serve with a dollop of sour cream, yogurt, or whipped cream, if desired.

SIX SERVINGS

IRRESISTIBLE WINTER COMPOTE

RIDGEWAY HOUSE

LA CONNER, WASHINGTON

1¾ cups apple juice

¼ cup cranberry juice

½ cup pitted prunes

½ cup dried apricots

¼ cup raisins

¼ cup dried cherries (optional)

¼ cup bourbon

4 thin slices fresh lemon

¼ teaspoon ground ginger

1 tart apple, peeled, cored, and cut into thin wedges

1 pear, peeled, cored, and cut into thin wedges

11 ounces canned mandarin oranges, drained

1 tablespoon Grand Marnier liqueur

Granola and star fruit (optional)

In a large, heavy saucepan, heat juices with dried fruit; bring to a boil. Add bourbon, lemon slices, and ginger. Reduce heat to low; cover and simmer for 15 minutes. Add apple and pear wedges; simmer 5 to 7 minutes, until fruit is tender. Add mandarin oranges and liqueur. Remove from heat. Spoon into individual dishes. Sprinkle with granola and garnish with star fruit, if desired. Can be served warm or cool.

SIX SERVINGS

HAZELNUT HONEY BUTTER

McGILLIVRAY'S LOG HOME BED & BREAKFAST

ELMIRA, OREGON

¼ cup butter, softened

1 cup honey, at room temperature

1 teaspoon vanilla extract

¼ cup chopped hazelnuts (filberts)

With an electric mixer or food processor, whip together butter, honey, and vanilla extract; add nuts. (Nuts can be chopped quickly in a blender.) Store butter covered in refrigerator. Serve with pancakes, waffles, or muffins.

APPROXIMATELY 1½ CUPS

CRANBERRY BUTTER

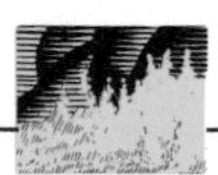

1 pound butter, softened

½ cup coarsely chopped raw cranberries

½ cup packed brown sugar

¼ cup honey

¼ cup ground walnuts

½ cup cranberry sauce

1 tablespoon grated orange rind

1 teaspoon grated lemon rind

2 tablespoons buttermilk (optional)

With an electric mixer or food processor, whip butter at high speed until pale yellow. Add cranberries, brown sugar, honey, walnuts, cranberry sauce, and orange and lemon rind. Add 1 tablespoon buttermilk, if desired. Whip at medium speed until light pink. Note: Butter can be frozen. Thaw, and then whip with 1 tablespoon buttermilk before serving. Serve with pancakes, waffles, or muffins.

APPROXIMATELY 3 CUPS

FLUFFY MAPLE SPREAD

BEACONSFIELD BED & BREAKFAST

VICTORIA, BRITISH COLUMBIA

½ cup butter, melted

½ cup maple syrup

2 cups confectioners' sugar

1 egg, separated

Chopped walnuts (optional)

In a blender or food processor, combine butter and maple syrup. In a medium bowl, using a hand mixer, beat sugar with syrup mixture. Add egg yolk and continue to beat. Add egg white and beat until smooth. Garnish with chopped walnuts. Serve with pancakes, waffles, or French toast.

EIGHT SERVINGS

HUCKLEBERRY-RHUBARB JAM

MARIANNA STOLTZ HOUSE

BED & BREAKFAST

SPOKANE, WASHINGTON

1½ cups crushed huckleberries

¾ cup cooked, mashed rhubarb

3½ cups sugar

3-ounce pouch liquid pectin (such as Certo)

In a large Dutch oven, combine huckleberries, rhubarb, and sugar; mix well. Place over high heat and bring to a full boil. Boil for 1 minute, stirring constantly. Remove from heat and stir in pectin. Alternately stir and skim for 5 minutes; discard floating fruit. Ladle into hot, sterilized jars and seal.

4½ CUPS

ORANGE-GINGER SAUCE

THE LOOKOUT

BED 'N BREAKFAST

NANOOSE BAY, BRITISH COLUMBIA

2 tablespoons peeled, minced fresh ginger

½ teaspoon grated orange rind

½ cup orange juice

½ cup water

2 tablespoons light corn syrup

1 cup sugar

In a small saucepan, combine ginger, orange rind, orange juice, water, corn syrup, and sugar. Bring to a boil, uncovered. Boil for 5 minutes over medium-high heat. Serve over pancakes, waffles, or French toast.

1½ CUPS

APPLE CIDER SYRUP

HILLTOP BED & BREAKFAST

FERNDALE, WASHINGTON

1 cup sugar

2 tablespoons cornstarch

½ teaspoon pumpkin pie spice

2 cups apple cider

2 teaspoons lemon juice

¼ cup butter

In a saucepan, mix sugar, cornstarch, and pumpkin pie spice. Add apple cider, lemon juice, and butter. Cook over medium heat, stirring frequently, until thick. Serve warm over pancakes or waffles.

APPROXIMATELY 2 CUPS

BLACKBERRY SYRUP

MOON & SIXPENCE

FRIDAY HARBOR, WASHINGTON

2 cups fresh blackberries

¼ cup sugar

½ cup orange juice

In a saucepan, combine berries, sugar, and orange juice. Cook over medium heat for 5 minutes. Lower heat when sauce begins to simmer; continue cooking for about 15 minutes. Serve warm over pancakes, waffles, or ice cream.

APPROXIMATELY 2 CUPS

BREAKFAST SALSA

4 cloves garlic, finely minced

2 tablespoons olive oil

2 jalapeño peppers, seeded and finely chopped

1 green pepper, chopped

½ red onion, finely chopped

2 pounds fresh ripe tomatoes, peeled and quartered

¼ cup red wine

3 tablespoons finely chopped parsley

¼ cup finely chopped fresh cilantro

6 ounces tomato paste

1 teaspoon ground cumin

½ teaspoon fresh cracked peppercorns

½ teaspoon cayenne pepper (optional)

In a medium saucepan, sauté garlic in olive oil until golden brown. Add peppers and onion and sauté briefly. Add tomatoes and wine; reduce heat and stir until well blended and heated through. Add parsley and cilantro; remove from stove. Stir in tomato paste, cumin, cracked pepper, and cayenne, if desired. Refrigerate. Serve chilled with eggs or potatoes.

SIX CUPS

PEACH SMOOTHIE

PALMER HOUSE

BED & BREAKFAST INN

LINCOLN CITY, OREGON

8 large, ripe peaches, peeled and chopped

Juice of 2 large oranges

½ cup honey

½ cup crème fraîche or sour cream

Kiwi slices or mint sprigs (optional)

In a blender or food processor, puree the peaches until smooth; add freshly squeezed orange juice and mix thoroughly; add honey and blend completely. Add crème fraîche and mix until well blended. Pour into 6 glasses. Garnish with kiwi slices or mint sprigs, if desired. Serve immediately.

SIX SERVINGS

CITRUS COOLER

STANGE MANOR

BED & BREAKFAST

LA GRANDE, OREGON

1 cup cold milk

½ cup orange juice

1 orange, peeled and quartered

1 lemon, peeled and quartered

1 tablespoon sugar

4 ice cubes

Put milk, orange juice, orange, lemon, sugar, and ice in blender or food processor; liquefy for 45 seconds, or until smooth. Pour into glasses and serve immediately.

APPROXIMATELY THREE SERVINGS

DELICIOUS DATE SHAKE

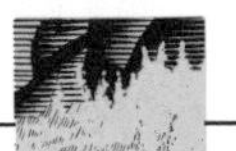

WILLCOX HOUSE

BED & BREAKFAST

CAMANO ISLAND, WASHINGTON

⅓ cup pitted whole dates

½ cup orange juice

1 pint vanilla ice cream

½ cup plain yogurt

1 teaspoon instant coffee crystals (optional)

In a blender or food processor, combine dates and orange juice and blend until smooth. Add ice cream, yogurt, and coffee crystals, if desired, and process until well blended. Pour into chilled Champagne glasses. Serve immediately.

TWO SERVINGS

BREADS

PUMPKIN GINGERBREAD

3 cups sugar

1 cup vegetable oil

4 eggs

⅔ cup water

16 ounces canned pumpkin

2 teaspoons ground ginger

1 teaspoon each cinnamon, nutmeg, cloves, and allspice

3½ cups all-purpose flour

2 teaspoons baking soda

1½ teaspoons salt

½ teaspoon baking powder

Preheat oven to 350 degrees. In a large bowl, mix together sugar, oil, and eggs; add water. Beat in pumpkin and spices. In a medium bowl, sift together flour, baking soda, salt, and baking powder; add to pumpkin mixture and stir just until blended. Pour into two greased 5- by 9-inch loaf pans. Bake for 1 hour, until bread tests done.

TWO LOAVES

LEMON YOGURT BREAD

THE GREY WHALE INN

FORT BRAGG, CALIFORNIA

3 eggs

1 cup vegetable oil

1¾ cups sugar

2 cups lemon yogurt

1 tablespoon lemon extract

3 cups all-purpose flour

1 teaspoon salt

1 teaspoon baking soda

½ teaspoon baking powder

1 cup chopped almonds (optional)

Preheat oven to 350 degrees. In a large bowl, beat eggs. Add oil and sugar; blend well. Stir in yogurt and lemon extract. Sift together flour, salt, baking soda, and baking powder, and add to egg mixture. Stir in nuts, if desired, and mix just until blended. Spoon into 2 greased 5- by 9-inch loaf pans. Bake for 1 hour, until bread tests done.

TWO LOAVES

LEMON-HUCKLEBERRY BREAD

MIO AMORE PENSIONE

TROUT LAKE, WASHINGTON

⅓ cup butter, softened

1 cup sugar

3 tablespoons lemon extract

2 eggs

1½ cups all-purpose flour

1 teaspoon baking powder

1 teaspoon salt

8 ounces lemon yogurt

1 cup fresh or frozen huckleberries

GLAZE:

Juice of 1 lemon

½ cup sugar

Preheat oven to 350 degrees. Line bottom and sides of a greased 4- by 8-inch loaf pan with waxed paper. In a large bowl, cream together butter, sugar, and lemon extract. Beat in eggs. In a medium bowl, sift together flour, baking powder, and salt, and add to creamed mixture alternately with yogurt. Fold in huckleberries. Pour into prepared pan and bake for 50 to 60 minutes, until bread tests done. Remove from pan while still warm, and cool on a rack.

For glaze, combine lemon juice with sugar; brush over top of loaf.

Note: This bread is best when cut after 24 hours.

ONE LOAF

BARTLETT PEAR NUT BREAD

HERSEY HOUSE

ASHLAND, OREGON

3 eggs

1 cup vegetable oil

1½ cups sugar

½ teaspoon grated lemon rind

1 teaspoon vanilla extract

3 fresh Bartlett pears, peeled, cored, and chopped

3 cups unbleached flour

1 teaspoon salt

1 teaspoon baking soda

¼ teaspoon baking powder

1½ teaspoons cinnamon

Dash freshly ground nutmeg

⅔ cup chopped almonds

Preheat oven to 325 degrees. In a large bowl, beat eggs until light and fluffy. Add oil, sugar, lemon rind, vanilla extract, and chopped pears; mix well. Sift together flour, salt, baking soda, baking powder, cinnamon, and nutmeg; add to pear mixture and mix just until blended. Stir in almonds. Pour into 5 greased miniature loaf pans. Bake for 35 to 40 minutes, until bread tests done.

FIVE SMALL LOAVES

APPLESAUCE-RAISIN OAT BRAN BREAD

MOUNTAIN HOME LODGE

LEAVENWORTH, WASHINGTON

1 egg, beaten

1 cup applesauce

¼ cup butter, melted

½ cup granulated sugar

¼ cup packed brown sugar

1½ cups all-purpose flour

½ cup oat bran

2 teaspoons baking powder

¾ teaspoon salt

½ teaspoon baking soda

1 teaspoon nutmeg

½ teaspoon cinnamon

½ cup raisins

1 cup coarsely chopped walnuts

Preheat oven to 350 degrees. In a large bowl, mix together egg, applesauce, butter, and sugars. In a medium bowl, sift flour and combine with oatbran, baking powder, salt, baking soda, nutmeg, and cinnamon. Add to applesauce mixture, and mix until smooth. Fold in raisins and nuts. Bake in a greased 5- by 9-inch loaf pan for 1 hour, until bread tests done.

ONE LOAF

CINNAMON BREAD

TUCKER HOUSE

FRIDAY HARBOR, WASHINGTON

1 package active dry yeast

¼ cup warm water (105 to 115 degrees)

⅔ cup warm milk (105 to 115 degrees)

1 teaspoon salt

½ cup sugar

½ cup butter, melted and cooled

2 eggs

3 to 3½ cups all-purpose flour

1½ teaspoons cinnamon

ICING:

½ cup confectioners' sugar

1 tablespoon milk

½ teaspoon vanilla extract

Preheat oven to 350 degrees. In a large bowl, combine yeast and water; let stand until bubbly. Stir in milk, salt, ¼ cup of the sugar, and ¼ cup of the butter. Add eggs and 1½ cups of the flour; beat until smooth. Beat in the remaining 1½ to 2 cups flour. Turn dough over in a greased bowl; cover and let rise in a warm place until doubled (about 1 hour). Turn dough out onto a floured board and knead lightly, adding more flour as needed. Roll out into a 9- by 18-inch rectangle. Brush with 2 tablespoons of the butter. In a small bowl, mix the remaining ¼ cup sugar with cinnamon; sprinkle over dough. Roll up tightly. Turn loaf over and pinch seam together to seal. Put shaped loaf into a greased 5- by 9-inch loaf pan. Brush top with remaining 2 tablespoons butter. Cover and let rise until almost doubled (about 45 minutes). Bake for 30 to 35 minutes, until loaf is nicely browned and sounds hollow when tapped. Turn loaf out of pan onto cooling rack. For icing, in a small bowl, stir together confectioners' sugar, milk, and vanilla extract. While bread is still warm, drizzle icing over top and let run down sides. Cool before slicing.

ONE LOAF

ZUCCHINI CHOCOLATE BREAD

THE VICTORIAN BED & BREAKFAST

COUPEVILLE, WASHINGTON

3 eggs

1 cup vegetable oil

2 teaspoons vanilla extract

2 cups sugar

3 cups grated zucchini

2⅓ cups all-purpose flour

½ cup unsweetened cocoa

2 teaspoons baking soda

1 teaspoon cinnamon

1 teaspoon salt

¼ teaspoon baking powder

½ cup chopped nuts

½ cup chocolate chips

Preheat oven to 350 degrees. In a medium bowl, mix together eggs, oil, vanilla extract, sugar, and zucchini. In a large bowl, combine flour, cocoa, baking soda, cinnamon, salt, and baking powder; stir in nuts and chocolate chips. Add zucchini mixture to dry ingredients. Pour into 2 greased 5- by 9-inch loaf pans. Bake for 45 minutes, until bread tests done.

TWO MEDIUM LOAVES

BANANA-NUT BREAD

WESTWINDS BED & BREAKFAST

FRIDAY HARBOR, WASHINGTON

⅓ cup shortening or margarine

⅔ cup sugar

2 eggs

1 pound (3 to 4) ripe bananas, mashed

1¾ cups all-purpose flour

2¾ teaspoons baking powder

½ teaspoon salt

1 cup chopped pecans

Preheat oven to 350 degrees. In a large bowl, cream shortening. Add sugar and eggs; beat several minutes, until light and fluffy. Add mashed bananas; blend well. In a medium bowl, sift together flour, baking powder, and salt, and add to banana mixture. Fold in nuts. Mix just until blended. Turn batter into a greased 5- by 9-inch loaf pan. Bake for 60 to 70 minutes, until bread tests done.

Note: This bread keeps quite well when refrigerated.

ONE LOAF

CARROT-COCONUT BREAD

3 eggs

½ cup vegetable oil

1 teaspoon vanilla extract

2 cups finely shredded carrots

2 cups grated coconut

1 cup raisins

1 cup chopped walnuts

2 cups all-purpose flour

1 cup sugar

1 teaspoon baking soda

1 teaspoon baking powder

1 teaspoon cinnamon

½ teaspoon salt

Preheat oven to 350 degrees. In a large bowl, beat eggs until light. Stir in oil and vanilla extract. Add carrots, coconut, raisins, and nuts; mix well. In a separate bowl, sift together flour, sugar, baking soda, baking powder, cinnamon, and salt; add to egg mixture. Stir just until blended. Spoon into a greased 5- by 9-inch loaf pan. Bake for 1 hour, until bread tests done with a toothpick. Remove from pan and cool thoroughly. Note: Flavor and texture improve if loaf is wrapped and refrigerated for several days.

ONE LOAF

CRANBERRY BREAD

WHITE SULPHUR SPRINGS RANCH

CLIO, CALIFORNIA

2 tablespoons butter or margarine

1 egg

1 cup sugar

¾ cup orange juice

2 cups all-purpose flour

1 teaspoon baking powder

½ teaspoon baking soda

½ teaspoon salt

2 cups whole fresh cranberries

½ cup chopped nuts

Preheat oven to 350 degrees. In a large bowl, combine butter or margarine, egg, and sugar; mix well. Add orange juice, flour, baking powder, baking soda, and salt; stir just until moistened. Fold in cranberries and nuts. Bake in a greased 5- by 9-inch loaf pan for 60 to 70 minutes, until bread tests done.

ONE LOAF

MEXICAN CORN BREAD

PALMERS CHART HOUSE

DEER HARBOR, WASHINGTON

8-ounce can creamed corn

¾ cup milk

⅓ cup vegetable oil

1½ cups yellow cornmeal

2 eggs, lightly beaten

1 teaspoon baking powder

1 teaspoon salt

1 teaspoon sugar

½ teaspoon baking soda

1½ cups shredded Cheddar cheese

4-ounce can diced green chiles

Preheat oven to 375 degrees. In a large bowl, combine corn, milk, oil, cornmeal, eggs, baking powder, salt, sugar, baking soda, cheese, and chiles; blend well. Bake in a greased 8- by 11-inch baking dish for 30 minutes, until bread tests done.

EIGHT SERVINGS

QUICK IRISH SODA BREAD

GASLIGHT INN

SEATTLE, WASHINGTON

2 cups all-purpose flour

1 teaspoon salt

¾ teaspoon baking powder

¼ teaspoon plus pinch baking soda

1 to 1¼ cups buttermilk

Preheat oven to 375 degrees. In a medium bowl, combine flour, salt, baking powder, and baking soda. Stir in 1 cup of the buttermilk and mix well, adding more buttermilk as needed until dough pulls away from sides of bowl and forms a ball. Place dough on a floured surface and knead for 30 seconds. Shape into a round loaf. Place on a greased cookie sheet and, using a sharp knife, score a large X on top of the loaf. Bake for 45 minutes, until loaf sounds hollow when tapped.

ONE ROUND LOAF

HONEY WHEAT BREAD

CAMPBELL RANCH INN

GEYSERVILLE, CALIFORNIA

1½ cups boiling water

1 cup rolled oats

¾ cup honey

3 tablespoons butter or margarine, softened

2 teaspoons salt

1 package active dry yeast

2 cups warm water (105 to 110 degrees)

1 cup seven-grain cereal

3 cups whole wheat flour

4 cups all-purpose flour

Melted butter or margarine, for brushing tops

Preheat oven to 400 degrees. In a large bowl, pour the boiling water over the oats. Let stand 30 minutes. Add honey, butter or margarine, and salt to the oats. In a small bowl, dissolve the yeast in the warm water; add to oat mixture. Stir in cereal and then whole wheat flour. Add all-purpose flour to make a medium-soft dough. Turn onto a floured board and knead for 10 minutes, until smooth and elastic. Place dough in a greased bowl. Brush top with melted butter or margarine and cover with a towel. Let rise until doubled in bulk. Punch down and knead briefly. Divide dough into 6 equal portions. Shape into small loaves and place in 6 greased 3- by 5-inch loaf pans. Place the pans on a large cookie sheet, cover with a towel, and let rise until doubled. Bake loaves for 5 minutes. Reduce heat to 350 degrees and bake for 25 to 30 minutes longer, until loaves sound hollow when tapped. Remove bread from pans and place on cooling racks. Brush tops with melted butter or margarine. Best served warm. Note: Once cooled, these breads can be wrapped in foil and frozen.

SIX SMALL LOAVES

OATMEAL BREAD

COUNTRY WILLOWS

ASHLAND, OREGON

½ cup old-fashioned rolled oats

1 cup boiling water

2 tablespoons butter

¼ cup honey

1 package active dry yeast

¼ cup warm water (105 to 115 degrees)

1 cup milk

2 teaspoons salt

5 cups bread flour (approximately)

Melted butter, for brushing top

Preheat oven to 350 degrees. In a small saucepan, cook oats in boiling water for 5 minutes. Add butter and honey. Cool to lukewarm. In a small bowl, dissolve yeast in the warm water. Transfer oats to a large bowl, and add yeast mixture to oats. Mix in milk and salt. Add flour gradually to make a soft dough. Knead lightly. Shape into a loaf and place in a well-greased 5- by 9-inch loaf pan. Cover and let rise until doubled in bulk. Bake for 40 to 45 minutes, until loaf sounds hollow when tapped. Remove from oven, and brush top with melted butter.

ONE LOAF

CILANTRO BREAD

SANDLAKE COUNTRY INN

SANDLAKE, OREGON

4 cups all-purpose flour

1 cup rye flour

2 tablespoons active dry yeast

½ cup water (105 to 115 degrees)

2 cups cottage cheese

2 tablespoons butter

⅓ cup packed brown sugar

2 tablespoons minced onion

4 teaspoons chopped fresh cilantro

2 teaspoons salt

2 teaspoons baking soda

2 eggs

Preheat oven to 350 degrees. In a medium bowl, combine flours and set aside. In a large bowl, dissolve yeast in the warm water. In a small saucepan, heat cottage cheese and butter until lukewarm; add to yeast mixture. Add brown sugar, onion, cilantro, salt, baking soda, and eggs; mix well. Gradually add flours, beating after each addition. Batter should be stiff. Cover dough and let rise until doubled. Shape into two loaves. Place into two well-greased 5- by 9-inch loaf pans; let rise until doubled. Bake for 30 minutes, until loaves sound hollow when tapped.

TWO LOAVES

BRUNCH FOR ALL SEASONS

WINTER

Baked Cheese Omelet

Baked Potato Latkes (Pancakes)

Almond–Sour Cream Coffee Cake

Irresistible Winter Compote

Honey Granola

SPRING

Miniature Ham and Cheese Quiches

Apple-Filled Crêpes

English Tea Muffins

Swiss Muesli

Peach Smoothie

SUMMER

Scrambled Eggs with Smoked Salmon

Blackberry Cobbler

Sausage Strata

Poppy Seed Muffins

Citrus Cooler

FALL

Chile Cheese Bake

Breakfast Salsa

Corn Casserole

Cream Cheese Coffee Cake

Washington Baked Pears

MAKE IT SIMPLE

MAKE IT SPECIAL

January	Serve chilled red or white grape juice in champagne flutes—toast to the new year.
February	Bake heart-shaped muffins. Serve them warm with cranberry butter.
March	Arrive at a friend's doorstep with a breakfast basket in hand.
April	Whip butter with honey or grated orange peel for a gourmet spread.
May	Place fresh flowers into napkin rings to celebrate spring!
June	Prepare breakfast kabobs with chunks of cheddar cheese and fresh fruit (kids love them).
July	Serve yogurt parfaits on the Fourth. Layer yogurt with strawberries and blueberries. Top with star fruit.
August	Pack a breakfast picnic and take it to the beach.
September	Create your own gourmet coffee by adding cinnamon, cocoa, or flavoring to coffee before it is brewed.
October	Make breakfast, then go back to bed.
November	Bake pumpkin gingerbread. Be thankful.
December	Eat breakfast by candlelight.

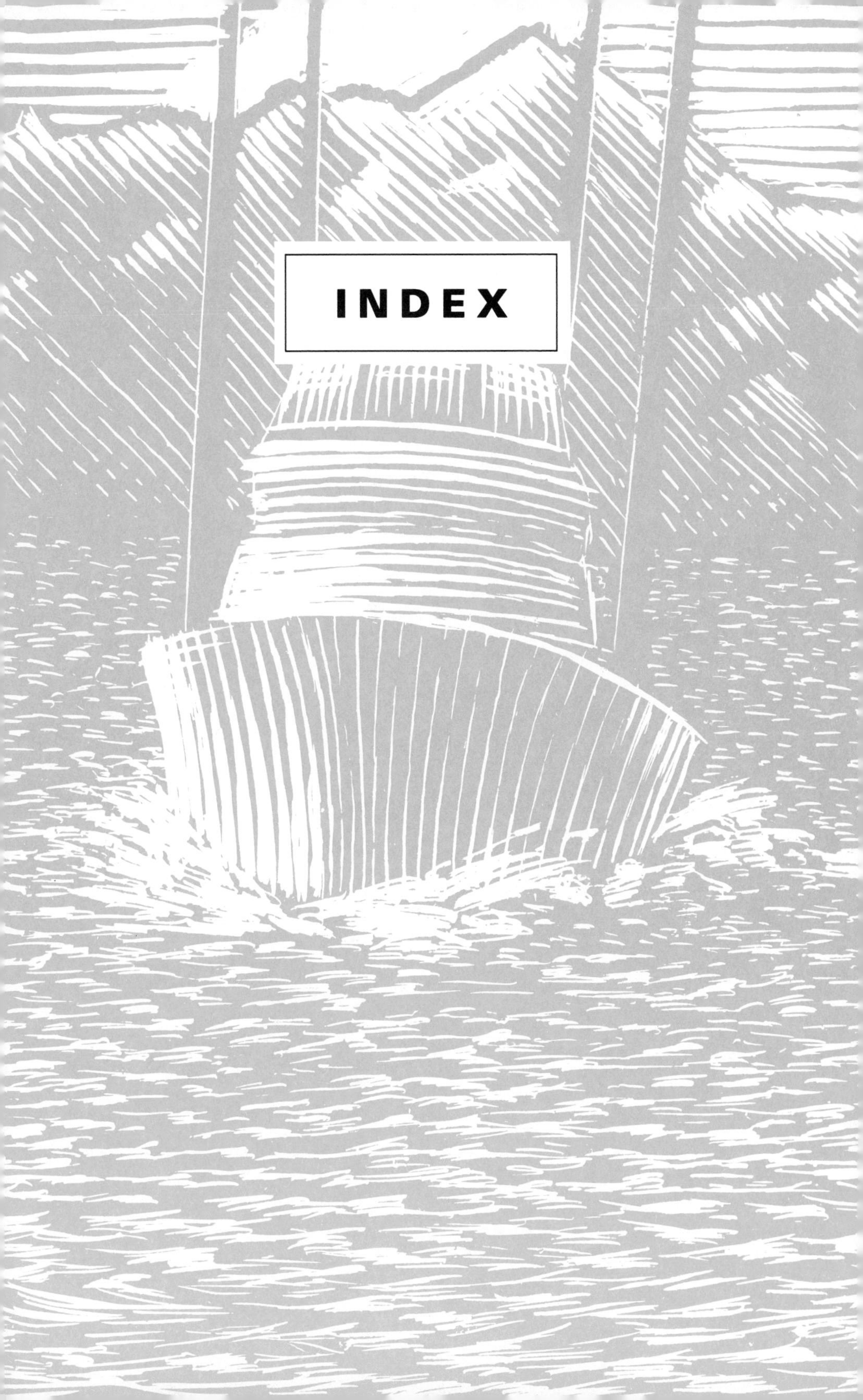

INDEX

A

B

C

D

E

F

G

H

J

K

L

M

N

O

P

Q

R

S

T

W

Z

ABOUT THE AUTHOR

Carol Frieberg is a fitness and nutrition consultant who has visited many bed-and-breakfast inns in the United States and Europe. Originally from the Midwest, she managed two bed-and-breakfast inns in Wisconsin, where she cooked both hearty country breakfasts and full-course weekend meals for winter guests. In 1988, she moved to Seattle to pursue her dream of having her own bed and breakfast. Since then, she has welcomed numerous friends and guests into her home. Many unknowingly became taste testers for the recipes in this book. Breakfast is her favorite meal of the day.

DID YOU ENJOY THIS BOOK?